DATE DUE

AP 21 '98			
MY 12'98			

DEMCO 38-296

SEPARATING
POWER

SEPARATING
POWER

༅

Essays on the Founding Period

GERHARD CASPER

HARVARD UNIVERSITY PRESS

Cambridge, Massachusetts / London, England / 1997

Library of Congress Cataloging-in-Publication Data

Casper, Gerhard.
    Separating power: essays on the founding period / Gerhard
Casper.
        p. cm.
    Includes index.
    ISBN 0-674-80140-7 (alk. paper)
    1. Separation of powers—United States—History. 2. United
States—Constitutional history. 3. United States—Politics and
government—1783–1809. I. Title.
KKF4565.C37 1997
320.473—dc20   96-36353

For Regina

CONTENTS

SEPARATING
POWER

1

THE TASK OF
SEPARATING POWER

Introduction

The separation of governmental powers along functional lines has been a core concept of American constitutionalism ever since the Revolution. Barren assertions of its importance, however, do not capture the complexity of the matter when viewed from the vantage point of either theory or practice. Philip B. Kurland has concluded: "The inefficacy of resorting to a general notion of separation of powers to resolve contests between two branches of government has long since been demonstrated by our history."[1] Kurland's "inefficacy" notwithstanding, the separation of powers has become a "rule of decision."[2] Especially over the last three decades, government actors, academic writers, and courts have vigorously debated the meaning of such labels as "legislative," "executive," and "judicial" as they face the conundrum of keeping the powers separate in a system of checks and balances.

1

This robust debate is anything but theoretical. And as the controversies over war powers, presidential impoundment of funds, executive privilege, the appointment of independent prosecutors, sentencing guidelines for federal judges, the legislative veto, and the independence of independent agencies, among others, demonstrate, the issues are hardly trivial. Peter L. Strauss commented back in 1984: "For the past few years the Supreme Court has been struggling with issues of government structure so fundamental that they might have been thought textbook simple, yet with results that seem to imperil the everyday exercise of law-administration."[3] Much of the energy has been focused on "an enduring (and angry) debate over the proper scope and extent of presidential power."[4]

In some sense, the controversy is as old as the country and certainly was lively during the presidency of Franklin D. Roosevelt. The current phase began more or less with claims of and for presidential power during the Vietnam era. Mythmakers advanced a constitutional mythology in which the role of Zeus was usually assigned to the President, who was seen as ruling with the aid of such abstractions as *the* executive power, *the* war power, *the* foreign affairs power, or *the* emergency power.[5] In 1964 McGeorge Bundy, special assistant for national security affairs in the Kennedy and Johnson administrations, referred to the President as "mankind['s] . . . Chief Executive for Peace."[6] Undifferentiated, all-inclusive executive power claims of this sort were, not surprisingly, met with wariness. While in the last decade, with the notable exception of the Iran-Contra affair, the strife has been mostly over whether there can be law execution or administration outside a "unitary" executive branch led by the President, the wariness that greeted the "imperial presidency"[7] continues to make itself felt.

As a sometime participant in the debate during the 1970s, I became increasingly concerned about the formalistic and often wooden manner in which disputants on all sides and in all three branches of government employed separation of powers notions to serve as premises for facile syllogisms. Furthermore, the authority of the framers of the Constitution was frequently invoked to declare these notions to have been "original" positions. Separation of powers wrangles thus became part of the larger methodological disputes over constitutional interpretation, the significance of "original meaning" and the importance to be attributed to "the intent of the framers." The fact that the Constitution does not even mention the separation of powers hardly served as a deterrent.

Anybody who attempts to keep up with the voluminous contemporary literature on the constitutional scope of presidential power faces the challenge of first having to choose among various approaches to constitutional interpretation. Perhaps surprisingly, there is a fair amount of agreement about the ultimate goal of such interpretation, at least as it concerns questions of the constitutional organization of the government. If one puts common-law approaches to constitutional interpretation to one side,[8] Lawrence Lessig and Cass R. Sunstein are right when they observe that "most practices of constitutional interpretation can be described as practices of fidelity—practices in which the commitments of the framers have a prominent place in finding and preserving constitutional meaning."[9] This agreement concerning "practices of fidelity," however, seems to result in a tendency to turn whatever differences do exist into fairly fierce theological disputes among the faithful.

Lessig and Sunstein's own commitment to interpretive fidelity very explicitly includes a broad consideration of context and contextual changes throughout our constitutional history,[10] while others follow a more or less elaborate, even rigid hierarchical approach that, for instance, sequentially considers the "plain meaning" of constitutional terms and resolves ambiguities by resorting first to contemporary "public" statements, then to "private" statements, and finally to postenactment history or practice.[11]

It is difficult, though, as constitutional history demonstrates, by no means impossible, to ignore the fundamental point that the meaning of constitutionalism is that the Constitution has meaning and that we must therefore understand and state it with as much fidelity as is humanly possible.[12] It would, of course, be unsound to ignore the historical fact that the Constitution has been adapted by Supreme Court interpretation and governmental practices to meet changing needs. Yet the fact of change (including "unconstitutional" change) does not mean that "anything goes," and fidelity to the framers' Constitution is not an all-or-nothing affair.[13]

However, the task of immersing ourselves in legal institutions and their historical background is laborious and the pitfalls are innumerable. For instance, it may be that the framers, in "vesting" legislative, executive, and judicial powers, had in mind a plain meaning of the verb "to vest" and, in this respect, phrased Articles I, II, and III of the Constitution with precision.[14] The difficulty is always that the normative importance we attribute to particular terms needs to be checked against a background context that tends to be messy, contradictory, and incomplete.[15] Textual and contextual analysis is not a science but a judgment call. That judgment is made even more problematic if one attempts to relate the constitutional text to the framers' "basic" normative commitments. Determining them (the question is "whose" commitments "when") is far from easy, and it is additionally dangerous to seek to remain faithful to those commitments under radically changed conditions, without attributing to the framers our own policy preferences.[16] "Originalism" is not for the fainthearted.

For a little more than a decade and a half I have served as a law school dean, provost, and now university president. Although these responsibilities have taught me much about how motives and purposes get attributed and how statements come to be overinterpreted (and silences misconstrued), they have not left me with enough time to continue active participation in the normative controversies concerning the separation of powers and methods of constitutional interpretation. However, I have continued to examine the question of what role separation of powers notions played as the framers' generation faced practical problems of governmental organization and the conduct of government. In this project I have consulted some of the secondary literature but focused mostly on primary sources. Assuming that my readers possess basic familiarity with the constitutional structure, I have also avoided rehearsing most details of the constitutional distribution of powers, the system of checks and balances, and a number of well-known historical controversies. Instead, my emphasis has been primarily, though by no means exclusively, on somewhat more obscure aspects of the problem that may illuminate some of the complexities inherent in the generality of the separation of powers "doctrine."

The chapters in this volume were conceived as essays and claim to be no more. Although the respective scope of legislative, executive, and judicial powers has once again become a matter of dispute, the aim of these essays is not to draw specific lessons from history. "[T]he essay," Felix Frankfurter once said, "is tentative, reflective, suggestive, contradictory, and incomplete. It mirrors the perversities and complexities of life."[17] These essays are not, however, without a point of view. They suggest that the very centrality of the separation of powers doctrine in the last quarter of the eighteenth century quickly produced a sharpened sense of its uncertainty as the "first constitutional generation" encountered specific tasks of governmental organization and statecraft. Indeed, the doctrine itself mirrored the complexities of life and its symbolisms. It was "tentative, reflective, suggestive, contradictory, and incomplete." It did not provide a clear-cut major premise for syllogisms concerning the organization of government. A review of early theory and practices suggests that we should be reluctant to tie separation of powers notions to their very own procrustean bed.

The Separation of Powers Doctrine during the Period of Constitution-Making

"A society in which the guarantee of rights is not assured, nor the separation of powers provided for, has no constitution." This stringent formulation is that of Article 16 of the French Declaration of the Rights of Man of 1789.[18] With respect to the separation of powers, it expressed what had become an almost sacred article of faith in the deliberations of the constitutional assemblies of the United States and France.[19] The French National Assembly of 1789 was unanimous in its support. This unanimity was made easier by the fact that the principle was not seen to entail a specific formula for distributing governmental functions. All Article 16 meant was that the exercise of governmental powers should not be concentrated in one hand.[20]

The reference to separation of powers as a fundamental normative principle[21] in bills of rights can also be found in American constitutions. Article VI of the Maryland Declaration of Rights of 1776 thus provided "[t]hat the legislative, executive and judicial powers of government, ought to be forever separate and distinct from each other."[22] Similar formulations appear elsewhere, for instance in the 1776 Virginia Bill of Rights. In its constitution, Virginia repeated its commitment to the separation of powers and elaborated: "The legislative, executive, and judiciary department, shall be separate and distinct, so that neither exercise the powers properly belonging to the other: nor shall any person exercise the powers of more than one of them, at the same time."[23]

When these words were written, the separation of execu-

tive and judicial, legislative and executive powers had been
the subject of ever-increasing attention on both sides of the
Atlantic for about 150 years. Harrington, Nedham, Locke,
Bolingbroke, Montesquieu, Blackstone, Rousseau, Sieyès,
Adams, Jefferson, and Madison are only some of the names
associated with this debate.[24] Their respective contributions
reflected diverse political, constitutional, and theoretical
concerns. It is therefore hardly surprising that, by the last
quarter of the eighteenth century, no single doctrine using
the label "separation of powers" had emerged that could
command general assent.

Invocation of the term "separation of powers" in bills of
rights, such as those of Maryland, Massachusetts, New
Hampshire, North Carolina, Virginia, and France, however, suggests a common linkage between the concept of
liberty and the notion of separation of powers.[25] Although
the meaning of liberty was not something on which agreement existed, the functional linkage was emphasized again
and again. Montesquieu, perhaps the most frequently cited
and the most confused and confusing of the writers on
separation of powers, provided the classical formulation
concerning the linkage:

> When the legislative and executive powers are united
> in the same person, or in the same body of magis-
> trates, there can be then no liberty; because apprehen-
> sions may arise, lest the same monarch or senate
> should enact tyrannical laws, to execute them in a
> tyrannical manner.
>
> Again, there is no liberty, if the power of judging be

not separated from the legislative and executive. Were it joined with the legislative, the life and liberty of the subject would be exposed to arbitrary control; for the judge would be then the legislator. Were it joined to the executive power, the judge might behave with violence and oppression.[26]

As put forward by Montesquieu, separation of powers is a functional concept. Separation is a necessary, if not sufficient, condition of liberty: its absence promotes tyranny.

Unfortunately, many political writers, Montesquieu included, tended to amalgamate (and thus obscure) separation of powers notions with another possible condition of liberty, or at least of good government: the institution of "mixed" government, which was aimed primarily at balancing different classes or interests.[27] Since the days of Aristotle it had become customary to differentiate among forms of government, especially monarchy, aristocracy, and what we now refer to as democracy. The Greek historian Polybius hypothesized that Rome had avoided the cycle of change and deterioration occurring in states with a single form of government; instead, Rome had combined the three types of government to create a state of equilibrium through the principle of counteraction.[28] Although Polybius' analysis of the Roman constitution was less than convincing, he firmly established the notion of mixed government that eventually became commonplace,[29] especially as applied to the British constitution and as advocated by Montesquieu and John Adams, among others. Adams thought that Polybius' views

9

were "deservedly revered."[30] After a detailed account of those views, however, Adams suggested that Polybius was wrong in judging that the invention of a more nearly perfect system of government than the Roman one was impossible: "We may be convinced that the constitution of England, if its balance is seen to play, in practice, according to the principles of its theory—that is to say, if the people are fairly and fully represented, so as to have the power of *dividing or choosing, of drawing up hill or down,* instead of being disposed of by a few lords—is a system much more perfect. The constitutions of several of the United States, it is hoped, will prove themselves improvements both upon the Roman, the Spartan, and the English commonwealths."[31] The debate about the desirability of mixed government thus concerned issues of immediate relevance to the American revolutionaries: the manifestations of British constitutional arrangements in the governmental structures of the former colonies and ways to improve them.

Although great differences existed in the institutional arrangements of government in the various colonies,[32] to say that, by and large, the colonies had "mixed" government based on the British model, with monarchic, aristocratic, and democratic elements manifested in their governors, councils, and legislatures, is not an exaggeration. A London compendium from 1755 said of the colonial governments: "By the governor, representing the King, the colonies are monarchical; by a Council they are aristocratical; by a house of representatives, or delegates from the people, they are democratical."[33]

This summary of mixed government, more an "ideal

type" than a complete description of the constitutional facts, did not mean that separation of powers notions were absent before 1776. Rather, they were intertwined with older notions reflecting the allocation of powers in the mixed colonial regimes.[34] In these mixed regimes, only the popular house of the legislature represented the people; the often predominating gubernatorial powers possessed legislative, executive, and judicial elements; and the functionally differentiated judiciary was kept less than completely separate. Although the colonists and the colonial legislatures were in fact highly autonomous in relation to London, governmental authority that depended on London differed sharply from governmental authority whose source was essentially local.

The challenge faced after the Declaration of Independence was how to adapt the institutions of mixed government to the doctrine of popular sovereignty.[35] The issue was no longer the separation of differently based powers, but the separation of power (in the singular) flowing from one source: the people. If the separation of powers was a necessary condition of liberty, the task was to reconcile it with the notion of popular sovereignty, which was invoked explicitly and dramatically in the majority of the new state constitutions and which was itself the foremost expression of that liberty.

Given the suddenness of the change in governance, the task of dividing power into different elements was truly formidable. As Gordon Wood has written: "Overnight modern conceptions of public power replaced older archaic ideas of personal monarchical government . . . As sovereign expressions of the popular will, these new republican governments acquired an autonomous public power that their monarchical predecessors had never possessed or even claimed . . . In other words, did it any longer make sense to speak of negative liberty where the people's positive liberty was complete and supreme?"[36] What did it mean to protect the people as citizens from the people as rulers?[37] Were the institutions of government to be hierarchically structured? If power was to be separated into powers, should they be rejoined in a system of checks and balances?[38]

A further problem was the stratification of the people in the former colonies: there were old inhabitants and newcomers, revolutionaries and loyalists, free men and indentured servants and slaves. "Americans liked now to think of themselves as a society without rank. Yet they had always distinguished the 'better sort' among them from the 'middling sort' and from the 'poorer sort.' "[39] Often there was a "gentry" as distrustful of the "people" as the "people" were distrustful of the "gentry." The tensions resulting from these stratifications were bound up with the organizational tasks of the new states.

The Separation of Powers in State Constitutions

As one reviews the state constitutions adopted between 1776 and 1787 for the ways in which they implemented separation of powers notions, it is striking that the particulars display an exceedingly weak version of separation of powers. Most of the constitutions made a conceptual distinction, either explicitly or implicitly, among legislative, executive, and judicial functions, introduced more or less elaborate systems of interbranch ineligibilities, and gave some, though often a modest, measure of independence to the judiciary.

The most distinct feature of the constitutions, however, was the dependence of the executive on the legislative branch on four counts. First, only New York, Massachusetts, and New Hampshire provided for the election of governors by voters. In the latter two states, the choice reverted to the legislature if no candidate received a majority of the votes. The other constitutions granted the legislature the power to elect the governor or president, typically on an annual basis. In Pennsylvania the legislature and the "supreme executive council," which was popularly elected, jointly chose the president. Second, only Massachusetts and New York recognized an overridable veto.[40] In New York the veto power was lodged in a council of revision. Third, all states provided for some kind of executive or privy council, generally elected by the legislature.[41] Fourth, states distributed the power of appointments in various ways, but legislative controls predominated.

Furthermore, although governors were authorized to exercise, subject to council participation, "the executive powers of government," this authorization was occasionally restricted by the clause that the exercise of executive powers had to be done according to the laws of the state.[42] Virginia added the proviso that the governor "shall not, under any pretence, exercise any power or prerogative, by virtue of any law, statute or custom of England."[43]

The 1776 state constitutional arrangements met with

some immediate criticism on separation of powers grounds. In 1777 New York provided for more separation, and the 1778 draft constitution of Massachusetts was rejected, partially because it was viewed as insufficiently mindful of the separation of powers. The towns of Essex County, in the so-called Essex Result of 1778, submitted a detailed critique that not only deplored the lack of "proper" executive authority but also disapproved of the intermingling of executive, legislative, and judicial powers.[44]

The Essex Result considerably complicated the debate over separation of powers by invoking the notion of checks and balances. "A little attention to the subject will convince us, that these three powers ought to be in different hands, and independent of one another, and so ballanced, and each having that check upon the other, that their independence shall be preserved."[45] The insight that checks and balances were needed to maintain the independence of each of the three branches revived the concept of balanced government without quite capturing the complexity of the matter. The problem had primarily become that of separation of power flowing from a single source, rather than the balancing of various factions in the organization of the government. In its newly added Bill of Rights, the 1780 constitution of Massachusetts addressed the principle explicitly in language that can also be found in the earlier state constitutions: "All power residing originally in the people, and being derived from them, the several magistrates and officers of government, vested with authority, whether legislative, executive, or judicial, are their substitutes and agents, and are at all times accountable to them."[46]

In the end, the 1780 Massachusetts Constitution was not dramatically different from the 1778 draft in the manner in which it distributed powers, although the later document did provide for the (overridable) gubernatorial veto. Its main balancing feature could already be found in the 1778 draft: the annual election of the governor directly by the voters (provided a candidate received a majority of votes). The separate gubernatorial election was, of course, in accord with John Adams' strong belief in an executive "distinct and independent of the legislative."[47]

The Bill of Rights of the 1784 New Hampshire constitution expressed clearly that the doctrine of separation of powers, or for that matter the notion of checks and balances, could not supply neat formulas from which proper governmental organizational arrangements would follow automatically. Article XXXVII of the New Hampshire Bill of Rights displayed a deeper appreciation of the problem than the more barren assertions in all the other state constitutions: "In the government of this state, the three essential powers thereof, to wit, the legislative, executive and judicial, ought to be kept as separate from and independent of each other, as the nature of a free government will admit, or as is consistent with that chain of connection that binds the whole fabric of the constitution in one indissoluble bond of union and amity."[48]

This provision, which is still in force, obviously views the separation of powers as essential to free government. However, it also reflects the concept of separate and independent powers as limited by the very notion of free government and by the necessity of maintaining "the whole fabric of the constitution." In short, New Hampshire emphasizes separation, coordination, and cooperation. Its dialectical view of the matter concisely summarizes the difficulties that awaited the federal constitutional convention as it faced the separation of powers "doctrine."

The Transition from the Articles of Confederation to the Federal Constitution

The Articles of Confederation had established a congress of state delegates as the central lawmaking and governing institution. Although its president, committees, and civil officers partook of an executive quality,[49] and although after 1780 it established a court of appeals for cases of capture,[50] one can hardly view the Confederation as possessing the characteristics of a tripartite government. On the other hand, one should not overlook the fact that some institutional separation of administrative tasks had evolved, dictated, as it were, by the nature of things and by the need to free the Congress from concerning itself with too much administrative detail.[51]

Although the absence of separation of powers was not generally viewed as the main weakness of the Confederation, Hamilton criticized the Articles as early as July 1783 for "confounding legislative and executive powers in a single body" and for lacking a federal judicature "having cognizance of all matters of general concern."[52] In a draft resolution calling for a convention to amend the Articles, Hamilton wrote that the Confederation's structure was "contrary to the most approved and well founded maxims of free government which require that the legislative executive and judicial authorities should be deposited in distinct and separate hands."[53] Hamilton had intended to submit the resolution to the Continental Congress, but abandoned the project for want of support.[54]

When John Randolph opened the substantive deliberations of the 1787 Convention with his enumeration of the defects of the Confederation, he apparently made no reference to separation of powers.[55] The Virginia Plan, submitted the same day, however, implied separation of powers and called for a quadripartite governmental structure: a bicameral legislature, a national executive, a national judiciary (to serve during good behavior), and a council of revision to be composed of the executive and members of the judiciary. The first house of the legislature was to elect the second from a pool of candidates to be nominated by the states, and the legislature was to elect the executive and judiciary. The executive was to enjoy "the Executive rights vested in Congress by the Confederation," but what these rights were was not adumbrated.[56]

Other plans for a constitution all presupposed a three-branch structure of government.[57] On May 30, the day following submission of the Virginia Plan, the Committee of the Whole adopted overwhelmingly a resolution "that a national government ought to be established consisting of a supreme Legislative, Judiciary, and Executive."[58] In a way, this event was the beginning and the end of the consideration of separation of powers *as such* in the Convention. To be sure, in the subsequent discussions of the structure and powers of the legislative, executive, and judicial branches as well as in the repeated debates concerning a council of revision, the delegates raised many points about the independence of the respective branches, the dangers of encroachments, and the need for checks and balances. What was strikingly absent, however, was anything that one might view as a coherent and generally shared idea of separation of powers.

The constitutional text itself, though implying the notion of distinct branches, did not invoke the separation of powers as a principle. Some of the state ratifying conventions attempted to remedy this omission in their original proposals for bills of rights to be added to the Constitution. Madison also sought a remedy. In 1788, in *The Federalist Papers,* Madison had considered it necessary to defend the Constitution against the charge that it paid no regard to the separation of powers. His core argument in *The Federalist No. 47* was the "impossibility and inexpediency of avoiding any mixture" as demonstrated by the state constitutions and as supported by the "oracle who is always consulted and cited on this subject . . . the celebrated Montesquieu." Montesquieu, according to Madison, did not mean to suggest that the three departments "ought to have no *partial agency* in, or no *control* over, the acts of each other."[59]

Madison's 1789 proposal for a constitutional amendment to incorporate the separation of powers formally into the federal Constitution was ingenious in the manner in which it formulated a separation of powers doctrine that took account of the constitutional scheme of checks and balances: "The powers delegated by this constitution, are appropriated to the departments to which they are respectively distributed: so that the legislative department shall never exercise the powers vested in the executive or judicial; nor the executive exercise the powers vested in the legislative or judicial; nor the judicial exercise the powers vested in the legislative or executive departments."[60] The separation of powers provision of Roger Sherman's draft bill of rights, also dating from the summer of 1789, captured even more clearly the point made by Madison's proposed article VII: "The legislative, executive and judiciary powers vested by the Constitution in the respective branches of the Government of the United States shall be exercised according to the distribution therein made, so that neither of said branches shall assume or exercise any of the powers peculiar to either of the other branches."[61]

The House adopted Madison's amendment (with a minor change) despite objections that it was unnecessary and "subversive of the Constitution."[62] Madison supposed "the people would be gratified with the amendment, as it was admitted that the powers ought to be separate and distinct; it might also tend to an explanation of some doubts that might arise respecting the construction of the Constitution."[63] This was an intriguing suggestion: the amendment would provide a principle of interpretation for the Constitution—*in dubio, pro* separation of powers. In fact Madison had taken this position earlier in the year when discussing the removal power.[64] Alas, the Senate rejected the amendment for reasons we shall never know.[65] One can only surmise that the Senate was not eager to adopt separation of powers as an independent doctrine or even as a mere principle of construction for the many and subtle "mixing" decisions of the framers, some of which benefited the Senate.

With regard to these "mixing" decisions, on such crucial touchstones as the mode of selecting the President and the assignment of the appointments power, the Convention delegates could not agree on constitutional solutions until the very end of their deliberations. Only the presidential veto (with the two-thirds override) stood more or less firm from the very beginning of the Convention,[66] although for most of its duration it was thought to be vested in a President who would be elected by the legislature.[67] Convention delegates twice defeated proposals for an absolute veto but agreed upon a three-fourths override on August 15, until reconsideration of the matter on September 12.[68]

As to the mode of selecting the President, election by the legislature was more or less supported firmly until, at the end of August, the issue became clearly linked to that of state power and influence. The electoral college compromise worked out by the Committee on Remaining Matters "almost satisfied almost everybody."[69] However, in the context and in light of what went on before, one should be reluctant to view the compromise as a ringing endorsement of a John Adams–type position on the executive.

The Virginia Plan had been silent about the appointments power with the exception of legislative election of judges. Early on, however, the appointment of judges was given to the Senate.[70] The delegates discussed the matter repeatedly, although, again, the division of the power into one of presidential nomination and Senate advice and consent came only as part of the compromises made by the Committee on Remaining Matters. The delegates overwhelmingly agreed to this division of the appointments power on September 7, after James Wilson had objected in vain to "blending a branch of the Legislature with the Executive."[71] Likewise, a joint ballot of both houses was to appoint the treasurer, and only on September 14 was this provision struck in the interest of conformity.[72]

One additional aspect of mixing deserves notice. In defense of his interpretation of the common defense and general welfare clause as a separate and substantive grant of power to the Congress, William Crosskey has argued that some of the congressional powers that appear in Section 8 of Article I were included there not to secure them as against the states but to prevent their passing to the President as executive prerogatives.[73] One need not agree with Crosskey's position on federal as against state powers to conclude that his argument has merit and has implications for the separation of powers doctrine. Commercial powers, the naturalization power, and the power to establish courts, subdue rebellions, make war, raise armies, or call out the militia were prerogatives that the delegates to the Convention did not hesitate to turn into legislative powers.[74] In doing so, they simply followed the prior example of the state constitutions.[75]

The Convention debates, taken as a whole, hardly suggest a strong consensus that the "[s]tate experience . . . contributed, nothing more strongly, to discredit the whole idea of the sovereign legislature, to bring home the real meaning of limited government and coordinate powers."[76]

21

Forrest McDonald, in his book on the origins of the Constitution, has concluded from the decisions of the Convention that the "doctrine of the separation of powers had clearly been abandoned in the framing of the Constitution."[77] This judgment presupposes that a doctrine existed that could be abandoned. Given the state of the discussion of the framers in the last quarter of the eighteenth century and the constitutions enacted after 1776, a "pure" doctrine of separation of powers can be no more than a political science or legal construct.[78]

No consensus existed as to the precise institutional arrangements that would satisfy the requirements of the doctrine.[79] The only matter on which agreement existed was what it meant not to have separation of powers: it meant tyranny. One should not belittle this insight. Madison and Sherman were right when, in their 1789 proposals, they claimed that the particular distribution of powers found in the Constitution could legitimately be seen as a version of an uncertain doctrine.[80]

2

THE CONDUCT OF GOVERNMENT
DURING THE WASHINGTON
ADMINISTRATION

*Communications between the Executive
and Legislative Branches*

Without any precedents under the new Constitution to follow, the Washington administration faced practical problems of governmental organization.[1] These problems were all the more challenging because the Constitution spoke about major formative issues only a little more clearly than it did about the separation of powers or the notion of checks and balances. Whether the subject was interbranch communications, the establishment of the "great departments" of government, or a foreign policy crisis in the Mediterranean, the President and Congress followed a course determined by a constantly evolving understanding of the appropriate conduct of government.

On April 30, 1789, President Washington took the oath of office and delivered his inaugural address before the

Congress. If Senator William Maclay is to be trusted, the President was exceedingly ill at ease;[2] but so was everybody else. Deciding the proper forms of address, whether titles were appropriate, what ceremonies the new government should conduct, and how the separate branches and the two houses of Congress should interact was not easy. Symbolism became important.

During the Senate debate that followed, the Vice President referred to Washington's address as "his most gracious speech."[3] This brought Maclay, a kind of republican prig, to his feet: "Mr. President, we have lately had a hard struggle for our liberty against kingly authority. The minds of men are still heated: everything related to that species of government is odious to the people. The words prefixed to the President's speech are the same that are usually placed before the speech of his Britannic Majesty. I know they will give offense. I consider them as improper. I therefore move that they be struck out."[4] And struck out they eventually were, over the protests of John Adams, who wanted "dignified and respectable government."[5] Dignified government also lost out when the House and Senate refused to grant the President a title such as "His Highness the President of the United States of America and Protector of the Rights of the Same."[6]

The importance of symbolism in the interaction between the branches was clear to many. Washington requested advice on these matters and wrote to Madison: "As the first of every thing, *in our situation* will serve to establish a Precedent, it is devoutly wished on my part, that these precedents may be fixed on true principles."[7]

24

In the context of separation of powers, physical interaction was an issue of surprising significance. How should messages be handled, what communications should be oral, which should be written, what was the proper mode for discussing oral communications? Some of these matters had been viewed as of such consequence for the separation of powers that state constitutions had regulated certain aspects of official intercourse. Article XXXII of the Georgia constitution of 1777, for instance, had provided that all transactions between the legislative and executive bodies be communicated by written message.[8] The underlying fear was that the executive might otherwise exercise undue influence on the deliberations of the legislature. As was so often the case, the reaction was against the British model of parliamentary government and what was perceived as ministerial predominance and corruption under that system.[9]

Four issues from the early days of the federal government are representative of the problems involved. The first concerned the Senate in its "executive" role regarding appointments. Should advice and consent be given *viva voce* or by ballot? In June 1789 the Senate decided to proceed by ballot in order to prevent "bargaining for" or "purchase of" votes.[10] The issue was reopened, however, after the Senate had, for the first time, rejected a presidential nomination in early August. Washington reacted with a message—one that was for him somewhat acerbic—in which he suggested that the senators might have asked him for more information concerning the candidate. The President then met with a Senate committee that proposed that he should communicate nominations orally, a step that might produce a *viva voce* vote. Washington insisted that it was up to the President to decide in what place and manner he should consult the Senate "as his council." Although he did not rule out personal appearance, he was firm about whose choice it was. The Senate yielded on presidential discretion and also changed its mind in favor of *viva voce* vote. Apparently, the President never made a nomination in person.[11]

Similar questions arose with respect to the Senate's role concerning treaties. On the very day on which the previous issue was resolved, Washington sent a message to the senators informing them that he would meet them in their chamber the following day "to advise with them on the terms of the treaty to be negotiated with the Southern Indians."[12] But Washington's attempt to consult in this way with the senators encountered two overwhelming difficulties. First, Washington's personal and official status made open and frank discussion very difficult. Second, even though Washington had brought the Secretary of War, General Henry Knox, along to answer questions about details, the treaty problems were simply too complex to be dealt with orally and without preparation. The Senate postponed the matter for the weekend and disposed of it on Monday, again with the President present.[13] The experiment was not repeated. The President continued to seek the Senate's advice in treatymaking, but he did so in writing.[14]

One of the more telling debates concerning modes of interaction occurred at the end of June in the House of Representatives. The House had before it the bill for establishing the Treasury Department, which made it the duty of the secretary to "digest and report plans for the improvement and management of the revenue, and the support of the public credit."[15] No similar clause was contained in the legislation establishing the Foreign Affairs and War Departments. Its presence here reflected the special constitutional role of the House with respect to bills for raising revenue: "It is the proper business of this House to originate revenue laws; but as we want information to act upon, we must procure it where it is to be had, consequently we must get it out of this officer, and the best way of doing so, must be by making it his duty to bring it forward."[16] This view of the matter was also that of the most likely appointee to the office, Alexander Hamilton, who wanted direct dealings with Congress and some independence from the President.[17]

The requirement to "report plans" met with strong objections. John Page of Virginia saw it as a "dangerous innovation upon the Constitutional privilege" of the House of Representatives. He worried that members would be inclined to defer to others who had thoroughly studied a case, and thus be subject to undue influence. "Nor would the mischief stop here; it would establish a precedent which might be extended, until we admitted all the ministers of the Government on the floor, to explain and support the plans they have digested and reported: thus laying a foundation for an aristocracy or a detestable monarchy."[18] Thomas Tucker of South Carolina used separation of powers language: "If we authorize him to prepare and report plans, it will create an interference of the Executive with the Legislative powers."[19] He referred the House to the mode of interaction specified by the Constitution in Section 3 of Article II—it was for the President to provide information and make recommendations. Other congressmen warned against "the doctrine of having prime and great ministers of State."[20] In the end, the House defeated the motion to strike out the provision but substituted the verb "prepare" for "report."[21]

The fourth significant example concerning modes of interaction occurred in 1792, when a host of substantive and symbolic issues arose. The House wanted to investigate the destruction of the U.S. Army under the command of General St. Clair at the hand of Indians in the Ohio country in 1791. The first proposal before the legislators was to request that the President institute an inquiry. This approach raised separation of powers objections. Although the reasons were more adumbrated than clearly stated, apparently the members believed that telling the President how to carry the laws into execution was an encroachment on executive power. The motion was overwhelmingly defeated, and instead a motion based on the powers of the House respecting the expenditures of public money was adopted. This adopted motion required the appointment of a House committee of inquiry that would "be empowered to call for such persons, papers, and records, as may be necessary to assist their inquiries."[22] In order not to encroach on executive power, then, the House proceeded to authorize the first parliamentary investigation of the executive branch.

The resolution was adopted on March 27, 1792. The committee then asked Secretary Knox for papers. Knox referred the matter to the President, who called together his cabinet. According to Jefferson, they were unanimous as to the power of the House to investigate. They also believed that requests for executive papers had to be made directly to the President, and that although the President should cooperate, he should refuse to deliver papers "the disclosure of which would injure the public."[23] The House accepted both restrictions when, on April 4, it passed a resolution "[t]hat the President of the United States be requested to cause the proper officers to lay before the House such papers of a public nature, in the Executive Department, as may be necessary to the investigation of the causes of the failure of the late expedition under Major General St. Clair."[24] This resolution treated the executive branch as a unitary "department" and recognized the potential need of the United States not to make everything public.[25]

After the committee report and public examination of such witnesses as Major General St. Clair and Secretary Knox, a resolution was introduced to notify the secretaries of Treasury and War that the House would consider the report "to the end that they may attend the House, and furnish such information as may be conducive to the due investigation of the matters stated in the said report."[26] Fisher Ames of Massachusetts supported the motion, noting the reputational interests involved. The motion "was due to justice, to truth, and to the national honor, to take effectual measures to investigate the business."[27] Ames saw the inquiry as preparatory to an impeachment. However, since the proceeding was not an impeachment at that time, opponents argued that the House had no right to cite the secretaries to appear before it while also urging "the impropriety of any of the Heads of Departments coming forward, and attempting in any way to influence the deliberations of the Legislature."[28] The latter reason seems to have been the weightier one.

Disputes concerning modes of interaction inevitably acquired partisan overtones as Congress began to develop parties. Arguments such as the ones just quoted reflected not only constitutional positions but also political interests. Congressmen sympathetic to the secretaries apparently favored their appearance before the House. Nevertheless, the House rejected the motion for a variety of stated reasons; among these, the impracticality of an investigation by the House as such figured prominently.

The vote led Secretary Knox to write to the Speaker asking for permission to appear before the House. Samuel Hodgden, who had been Quartermaster General during the poor provisioning of St. Clair's army, wrote a similar request. When the House discussed these requests, Madison suggested recommitment of the report to the select committee, which could then hear Knox and Hodgden. The House agreed to this, although Ames had argued strongly to provide an opportunity for vindication: "Shall they be sent to a Committee-room, and make their defence . . . in the hearing of perhaps ten or a dozen persons only?"[29]

The account of Madison's opposition to the motion to invite Secretaries Hamilton and Knox to appear before the House in the *Gazette of the U.S.* stated:

Mr. Madison objected to the motion on constitutional grounds, and as being contrary to the practice of the house. He had not, he said, thoroughly resolved the business in his own mind, and therefore was not prepared to state fully the effects which would result from the adoption of the resolution; but he would hazard thus much, that it would form an innovation in the mode of conducting the business of this house, and introduce a precedent which would lead to perplexing and embarrassing consequences; as it involved a conclusion in respect to the principles of the government, which, at an earlier day, would have been revolted from. He was decidedly in favour of written information.[30]

Although this summary is more suggestive than explicit, it shows at least that Madison viewed the personal appearance of cabinet members as involving the very "principles of the government" as they had emerged. What had emerged, as illustrated by the St. Clair episode in particular, was a mode of interaction to some extent at arm's length, although personal interaction was considered appropriate at the committee level. What also had emerged was the President's control of the executive branch and therefore of the information to be provided the legislature. In the cabinet meeting about the St. Clair investigation, only Hamilton had invoked, not implausibly, a more direct relation with the House.[31]

The issues of what information Congress was entitled to, and what conditions could be placed on its circulation, were more complex. Abraham Sofaer correctly observed that during the Washington presidency there existed a widely shared view that the President had some discretion in declining to furnish information, and that the President was extremely careful in exercising that discretion.[32]

The President also claimed the right to communicate with the Congress on a confidential basis. Although this exercise presented few difficulties with the early Senate, which until 1794 met behind closed doors, the House ordinarily met in public, and its debates were widely reported in newspapers. Nevertheless, the House occasionally went into closed session to receive confidential communications from the President. During the Second Congress this procedure was formalized into a standing rule providing that "whenever confidential communications are received from the President of the United States" the House was to be cleared during the reading and all debates.[33] This rule in effect granted the President control of an important aspect of the manner in which the House conducted its business. In 1793, during the consideration of American relations with the Barbary Powers, the matter was reopened, and it was argued that the rule violated the public's right to know: "secrecy in a Republican Government wounds the majesty of the sovereign people." The reply was "that because this Government is Republican, it will not be pretended that it can have no secrets."[34] Indeed, the journal secrecy clause in Article I, Section 5 of the Constitution supports the latter proposition. The Constitution did not commit the country to the free circulation of information at any price. Nevertheless, the problem was not secrecy as such, but the executive's control over House deliberations. On December 30, 1793, the House amended its rule to provide for two phases: closed door reading of confidential communications from the President and closed-door debate "unless otherwise directed by the House."[35]

What is striking in these early instances of interaction between the Congress and the executive branch is the care with which arguments were phrased and the appreciation, by both branches, of the precedent-setting nature of contemplated action. Indeed, precedents for the modes and conditions of communication were set that—for better or for worse—essentially endure to the present day. The separation of powers doctrine hardly compelled these precedents, yet the episodes display an inclination to maintain some distance between the legislative and executive branches in accord with their distinct responsibilities in a complex system of representative government. At the turn from the eighteenth to the nineteenth century this symbolic distancing was strengthened by the actual physical distance between the two branches in the new capital city.[36] However, as we shall see, the realities of the constitutional coordination of the governmental institutions in cases such as financial planning and foreign policy quickly overcame more barren notions of separation.

Establishment of the Departments of Government

William Maclay had this to say about the bills establishing the executive departments:

> [I do not] see the necessity of having made this business a subject of legislation. The point of view in which it has presented itself to me was that the President should signify to the Senate his desire of ap-

pointing a Minister of Foreign Affairs, and nominate
the man. And so of the other necessary departments.
If the Senate agreed to the necessity of the office and
the men, they would concur; if not, they would negative, etc. The House would get the business before
them when salaries came to be appointed, and could
thus give their opinion by providing for the officers or
not.[37]

Maclay's approach adapted to American constitutional
conditions the manner in which the great offices of state
had emerged in England—from the King's privy council:
the officers were created before the offices.[38] In the House
of Representatives, on the other hand, it was taken for
granted that the principles of organization for the executive
offices should be settled by legislation. The tenure of the
officers who would head the departments thus established
was the great separation of powers issue that overshadowed
all other issues in the spring of 1789. Its resolution has
become known as "the decision of 1789."[39]

Constitutional arrangements in the states had little relevance to the debate. The manner in which the state constitutions had dealt with appointments, terms of office, and
removal did not suggest a consensus of any kind.[40] In many
cases important officers were elected by the legislature for
one year or for more extended terms. Councils shared gubernatorial appointment powers that were subject to various legislative controls, including displacement. The
constitutions only occasionally included the phrase "service
during pleasure." No clear-cut state precedents were avail-

able to the members of the House of Representatives as they faced the task of interpreting the provisions of the U.S. Constitution with respect to the tenure of executive officers.

On May 19, after Elias Boudinot had introduced the subject, Madison moved that Congress establish departments of Foreign Affairs, Treasury, and War. The departments were to be led by secretaries, who were to be "appointed by the President, by and with the advice and consent of the Senate; and to be removable by the President."[41] The motion immediately focused attention on the location of the removal power. In the subsequent debate, two major issues emerged: (1) the substantive issue, and (2) the question whether Congress, especially the House of Representatives, should declare its views on the correct interpretation of the Constitution.[42]

Louis Fisher has rightly emphasized the wide-ranging nature of the debate, the complexity of the issues, and the shifting tide of opinion "that advanced and receded each day as the deliberation continued."[43] Nevertheless, the following major positions can be identified on the question of the location of the removal power:

1. Removal was possible only by means of impeachment.
2. The removal power belonged to the President because the Constitution did not provide otherwise and because the Senate was not expressly associated with it.
3. The removal power belonged to the President because it was an inherently executive power. The

Senate was a legislative body with only a qualified check upon the executive power.

4. The removal power belonged to the President because the President, under the Constitution, was answerable for the conduct of his officers.

5. The removal power was shared by the President and Senate because of its similarity to the appointment power, which was also shared.[44]

6. Congress could delegate the removal power to the President because of its power over offices and the terms of office.[45]

7. Congress had discretion in the matter on account of its powers under the necessary and proper clause.

The debate was replete with references to separation of powers. The views of James Madison and Michael Stone of Maryland respectively characterize two extremes. First, Madison's opinion:

Perhaps there was no argument urged with more success, or more plausibly grounded, against the constitution, under which we are now deliberating, than that founded on the mingling of the executive and legislative branches of the government in one body. It has been objected, that the senate have too much of the executive power even, by having a controul over the president in the appointment to office. Now, shall we extend this connection between the legislative and executive departments, which will strengthen the objection, and diminish the responsibility we have in the head of the executive? I cannot but believe, if gentlemen weigh well these considerations, they will think it safe and expedient to adopt the clause.[46]

Issues of constitutional power aside, Madison's position was clearly based on separation of powers notions. Stone considered such arguments as too late:

A separation of the powers of Government, between the Legislative, Executive, and Judicial branches, is considered as the proper ground for our opinion, and a principle which we must admit. Are we to get it brought into the Constitution? For I apprehend there is no such principle as a separation of those powers brought into the Constitution at present, but to the degree which an examination will appear to exist. Is there any express declaration, that it is a principle of the Constitution to keep the Legislative and Executive powers distinct? No. Has the Constitution in practice kept them separate? No. Whence is this idea drawn? That it is a principle in this Constitution, that the powers of Government should be kept separate? No sure ground is afforded for it in the Constitution itself. It is found in the celebrated writers on government; and, in general, I conceive the principle to be a good one. But if no such principle is declared in the Constitution, and that instrument has adopted exceptions, I think we ought to follow those exceptions, step by step, in every case to which they bear relation.[47]

In addition to questioning the significance of the separation of powers doctrine for the Constitution and the removal power, some members of the House doubted whether Congress should make any declaration regarding the allocation of constitutional powers. William Loughton Smith of South Carolina, who opposed presidential discretion to remove a department head, thought the issue should be left to the judiciary: "It will be time enough to determine the question when the President shall remove an officer in this way."[48] Elbridge Gerry, who believed in the similarity of the removal and appointments powers, wanted the clause "to be removable by the President" stricken, in part because he believed that the legislature should have no power to construe the meaning of the Constitution. He did assume that the judiciary had the power of exposition.[49] As far as the Congress was concerned, it could act only by amendment pursuant to Article V.[50]

In response to this proposition, Egbert Benson pointed out the impossibility of avoiding all construction of the Constitution. At the same time, he notified the House that he would move for new language in order to destroy all appearance that Congress was conferring the power of removal on the President. Such a conferral "would be admitting the House to be possessed of an authority which would destroy those checks and balances which are cautiously introduced into the Constitution, to prevent an amalgamation of the legislative and executive powers."[51]

On June 19 a motion to strike out the words "to be removable by the President" was defeated, 34 to 20.[52] On June 22 Benson introduced his amendment, which ingeniously was based on indirection. Specifically, it gave the chief clerk of the department the custody of all records "whenever the said principal officer shall be removed from office by the President of the United States, or in any other case of vacancy." The motion was carried, 30 to 18.[53] After its adoption, in accord with his previously announced plan, Benson moved to strike out the clause "to be removable by the President." The motion was carried, 31 to 19.[54] The "decision of 1789" was later sealed in an evenly split Senate, with the Vice President casting the decisive vote.[55]

Short of a roll-call analysis of the shifting alliances, which would be hampered by the facts that by no means all members of the House participated in the debates and that we have no reliable account of Senate proceedings, knowing how decisive the decision was and its exact meaning is difficult.[56] In any event, the real significance of the debate lies in the diversity of views expressed about the significance and meaning of separation of powers. In some way, most speakers, including Madison, recognized that distillation of a constitutional separation of powers doctrine that was supported by the constitutional text was difficult. This awareness led Madison and Benson to argue that "amalgamation" had been carried far enough and that doubtful cases should be resolved in favor of more separation and a more effective and responsible executive branch. Yet the contrary arguments were hardly frivolous, for they expressed a preference for construing the Constitution rather than relying on "celebrated writers on government."[57] Furthermore, how responsibility and efficacy could best be achieved in different contexts was by no means clear.

Madison himself provides a striking illustration of this last point. Only one week after the vote on the Benson motion, Madison rose in the House during the debate on the bill establishing the Treasury Department. The bill provided for a comptroller, whose duties included deciding, on appeal, without further review by the secretary, all claims concerning the settlement of accounts. The bill made no special provisions concerning the tenure of the comptroller. Madison, in analyzing the "properties" of the office, found them to be "not purely of an executive nature."

> It seems to me that they partake of a judiciary quality as well as executive, perhaps the latter obtains in the greatest degree. The principal duty seems to be deciding upon the lawfulness and justice of the claims and accounts subsisting between the United States and the particular citizens; this partakes strongly of the judicial character, and there may be strong reasons why an officer of this kind should not hold his office at the pleasure of the executive branch of the government . . .
>
> Whatever, Mr. Chairman, may be my opinion with respect to the tenure by which an executive officer may hold his office according to the meaning of the constitution, I am very well satisfied, that a modification by the legislature may take place in such as partake of the judicial qualities, and that the legislative power is sufficient to establish this office on such a footing, as to answer the purposes for which it is prescribed.[58]

Madison proposed tenure for a term of years, although, somewhat surprisingly after his opening words, he would still allow the President to remove the comptroller. The officer was to be reappointable. The point of the scheme was to establish the comptroller's dependence on the President through the removal power, on the Senate through reconfirmation, and on the House through impeachment and the power over his salary.[59]

Madison's intervention revealed the complexity of any classification scheme. Later in the debate he conceded that the office was neither executive nor judicial but "distinct from both."[60] Madison's intervention also showed that the views he had adumbrated at the beginning of the removal debate concerning congressional power over offices[61] were a function of the different organizational tasks confronted by the legislature.

Madison's rather unclear measure for protecting the comptroller against "interference in the settling and adjusting" of legal claims against the United States was seen by other members as, in Benson's words, "setting afloat the question which had already been carried"—service in the executive branch during pleasure.[62] In short, some feared that Madison had stirred up a hornets' nest, and the next day he withdrew the proposition.[63]

The real decisions of 1789 are those embodied in the statutes establishing the "great departments" of government. These statutes are of considerable interest beyond the fact that they recognized a presidential removal power. Three departments—Foreign Affairs, War, and Treasury— were established that were direct successors to those of the

Continental Congress. The departments of Foreign Affairs and War were denominated "executive" departments, and thus were placed squarely within the executive branch. Although areas of responsibility were spelled out, the secretaries were subjected explicitly to presidential directions: the principal officer "shall conduct the business of the . . . department in such manner as the President of the United States shall from time to time order or instruct."[64] The initial organization of the departments was skeletal, with only a chief clerk named expressly.

Matters were completely different with regard to the Department of Treasury. The Treasury was not referred to as an "executive" department, even though the Secretary of the Treasury was grouped with other "executive officers" in the act setting salaries[65] and the secretary was removable by the President. The legislation was silent on the subject of presidential direction yet did not vest the appointment of inferior officers in the secretary. An elaborate set of such officers and their responsibilities was spelled out in detail. The officers included an assistant secretary, a comptroller, an auditor, a treasurer, and a register, who were subjected to a detailed system of controls. For instance, disbursement could be made only by the treasurer, upon warrants signed by the secretary, countersigned by the comptroller, and recorded by the register.[66]

The duties of the secretary, as defined by the legislation, were extensive and involved direct relations with the Congress:

> Sec. 2. And *be it further enacted,* That it shall be the duty of the Secretary of the Treasury to digest and

prepare plans for the improvement and management of the revenue, and for the support of public credit; to prepare and report estimates of public revenue, and the public expenditures; to superintend the collection of the revenue; to decide on the forms of keeping and stating accounts and making returns, and to grant under the limitations herein established, or to be hereafter provided, all warrants for monies to be issued from the Treasury, in pursuance of appropriations by law; to execute such services relative to the sale of the lands belonging to the United States, as may be by law required of him; to make report, and give information to either branch of the legislature, in person or in writing (as he may be required), respecting all matters referred to him by the Senate or House of Representatives, or which shall appertain to his office; and generally to perform all such services relative to the finances, as he shall be directed to perform.[67]

As Forrest McDonald put it, "Hamilton could scarcely have asked for more."[68] Although we shall never know the exact influence that Hamilton had on the shape of the legislation, the direct link that the act created between the secretary and the Congress had ample state precedent. Even in New York, whose constitution was more generous than any other toward the executive branch, the treasurer was "appointed by act of the legislature, to originate with the assembly."[69] One should also recall that until September 14,

1787, the draft of the federal Constitution provided for the election of the treasurer.[70]

In the Congress, the Secretary of Treasury was seen as an indispensable, direct arm of the House in regard to its responsibilities for revenues and appropriations. The House had appointed a Committee of Ways and Means as early as July 24, 1789.[71] As soon as Hamilton was confirmed, the House turned the committee's task over to him and discharged the committee.[72] The House did not establish a standing Committee on Ways and Means until 1795.[73]

Whatever the constitutional significance of the different treatment accorded the Treasury Department, its symbolic significance for the separation of powers seems considerable. Only the departments of State and War were completely "executive" in nature. As to the Treasury, although Congress did not exclude the President from giving orders and instructions to its secretary, it claimed that authority for itself and did not even mention the President in this respect. This fact made presidential control of the secretary more tenuous, as Hamilton had been quick to point out when the cabinet discussed the proper response to the St. Clair inquiry. Congress certainly did not demand part of the power to execute the laws, but it varied the instruments for executing its own powers and those of the executive branch, in accordance with the subject matter to be regulated and its own sense of the legislature's responsibilities with respect to that subject matter. In other words, Congress stressed coordination rather than separation as it seemed constitutionally appropriate.

The Conduct of Foreign Relations:
The Algiers Problem

The perhaps best-known controversy concerning the conduct of foreign relations during the Washington administration is the battle over President Washington's Neutrality Proclamation of 1793 in the war between revolutionary France and Great Britain. Since the power to declare war is a congressional power, could the President commit the nation to peace?[74] When it came to questions concerning *enforcement* of neutrality, the debate included even the judicial branch, since the administration had decided to turn to the Supreme Court for advice on the legal implications of neutrality. Chief Justice Jay and the associate justices politely but firmly declined the request on separation of powers grounds.[75] Although it is tempting to take yet another look at the matter, I should like instead to turn to a more obscure foreign relations problem that raised and intertwined various aspects of the American version of the separation of powers.

"On the 25th of July, 1785, the schooner Maria, captain Stevens, belonging to a Mr. Foster, of Boston, was taken off Cape St. Vincents, by an Algerine corsair; and, five days afterwards, the ship Dauphin, captain O'Brien, belonging to Messieurs Irvins of Philadelphia, was taken by another Algerine, about fifty leagues westward of Lisbon. These vessels, with their cargoes and crew, twenty-one persons in number, were carried into Algiers."[76] With these words, Secretary of State Thomas Jefferson described an event that posed one of the most intractable foreign policy problems the new country encountered, one which would occupy the Washington administration throughout its eight years. The Algiers episode illustrates vividly the foreign policy issues that arise under a system characterized by a three-way (executive, Senate, House) allocation of decision-making authority. In evaluating its significance, one must keep in mind that one of the framers' central purposes in establishing the federal government was the effective and controlled conduct of foreign and defense policy.

Algiers, Tunis, and Tripoli were autonomous regencies of the Ottoman empire, governed by a local and regularly replenished military establishment of Turks and financed by tribute from country tribes, agricultural trade, and piracy. For the purposes of piracy, fleets of cruisers were maintained under Turkish sea captains. The piracy policy was one of declaring "war" on countries big and small, taking ships and seamen captive, putting the "slaves" to work, and then selling "peace." A fourth participant in these activities was Morocco, an independent state under a sultan. These four powers, the "Barbary Powers," exercised considerable control over Mediterranean and Atlantic shipping.[77] Because England withdrew her Mediterranean passes for American ships shortly after the outbreak of the War of Independence, the "American Revolution transferred from London to Philadelphia the problem of protecting American commerce."[78]

In 1784 the Continental Congress resolved to secure treaties with Morocco, Algiers, Tunis, and Tripoli. Indeed, a fifty-year treaty was concluded with Morocco in 1787.[79] However, negotiations with the other Barbary Powers collapsed, and the capture of the *Maria* and *Dauphin* exacerbated the problem.

The Continental Congress commissioned John Adams, Benjamin Franklin, and Thomas Jefferson to negotiate with the Barbary Powers. When these men sent an agent to Algiers, its ruler, the dey, demanded a $60,000 ransom. This sum amounted to more than $2,800 a head, considerably above the $200 that the commissioners had offered or the $550 that Jefferson was willing to pay in September 1788, when he employed the services of a French religious order to recover the hostages. In March 1790 Jefferson took up his new position of Secretary of State. The House of Representatives referred to the secretary a petition for relief concerning the American captives in Algiers.[80] At this point it becomes interesting to explore the manner in which the executive branch and Congress interacted to find a solution.

On December 30, 1790, the President sent both houses of Congress a report on the prisoners of Algiers which the House had requested. The Secretary of State had prepared the report for the President. On the same date Jefferson also sent the House a report on Mediterranean trade. The Secretary of State had prepared the latter report at the request of the House following the President's annual speech to his "Fellow Citizens of the Senate and House of Representatives" on December 8. In that address the President had called the congressmen's attention to the "distressful" state of the Mediterranean trade.[81]

Washington's cover letter accompanying the first report said: "I lay before you a report of the Secretary of State on the subject of the citizens of the United States in captivity at

Algiers, that you may provide on their behalf, what to you shall seem most expedient."[82] Jefferson's report consisted of a detailed account of diplomatic activities since the days of the Continental Congress, as well as of the "market" in Algerine captives—the per capita ransom paid by various European states. Jefferson stated somewhat laconically that from "these facts and opinions, some conjecture may be formed of the terms on which the liberty of our citizens may be obtained." He also pointed to the alternative of meeting force with force, suggesting the capture of Algerine mariners or, better still, Turks, for purposes of exchange. Jefferson concluded by emphasizing the connection of the subject matter at hand with "the liberation of our commerce in the Mediterranean."[83] The report was accompanied by extracts from diplomatic and other correspondence which had received some "judicious editing" by Jefferson.[84]

In response to a House request, Jefferson sent the report on Mediterranean trade directly to the House after the President had approved it. In his report Jefferson provided information about the importance of the Mediterranean ports for U.S. agricultural exports before the war. He stressed that navigation had not been resumed at all since the peace and discussed alternatives for coping with the situation, including the option "to obtain peace by purchasing it."[85] Jefferson relayed the opinion of a European source, "whose name is not free to be mentioned here," that the United States could not buy peace with Algiers for less than $1 million.[86]

Finally, Jefferson discussed "repel[ling] force by force" as an alternative. He provided estimates of the strength of the Algerine naval force, suggested that the United States needed a naval force equal to it, and put forward the idea of an alliance with other countries. He pointed to the fact that Portugal, by keeping a naval watch before the Straits of Gibraltar, had contained the Algerines within the Mediterranean. "Should Portugal effect a peace with them, as has been apprehended for some time, the Atlantic will immediately become the principal scene of their piracies." Jefferson concluded:

> Upon the whole, it rests with Congress to decide between war, tribute, and ransom, as the means of reestablishing our Mediterranean commerce. If war, they will consider how far our own resources shall be called forth, and how far they will enable the Executive to engage, in the forms of the constitution, the cooperation of other Powers. If tribute or ransom, it will rest with them to limit and provide the amount; and with the Executive, observing the same constitutional forms, to make arrangements for employing it to the best advantage.[87]

The report was so structured that Jefferson, while treating the alternatives fairly, made it clear where he stood (and, indeed, had stood all along): giving in to ransom demands would only encourage further extortion. This report too was accompanied by a range of diplomatic and other correspondence.[88]

Jefferson submitted the report with a request to the Speaker of the House that it be treated as a secret document because it was not in the interest of the United States that countries at peace with Algiers learn about American plans for concerted action. The galleries were indeed cleared, and the House forwarded the report to the Senate on a confidential basis.[89]

When the Senate received Jefferson's report on January 3, Maclay thought it breathed resentment and abounded "with martial estimates in a naval way."[90] Three days later, a Senate committee found that a naval force was necessary "and that it will be proper to resort to the same as soon as the state of the public finances will admit."[91] The committee was headed by Jefferson's friend John Langdon and included senators who were sympathetic to Hamiltonian trade policy.[92]

On February 1, 1791, the Senate adopted a resolution that the "Senate advise and consent that the President of the United States take such measures as he may think necessary for the redemption of the citizens of the United States now in captivity at Algiers, provided the expense shall not exceed forty thousand dollars; and, also, that measures be taken to confirm the treaty now existing between the United States and the Emperor of Morocco."[93] The last item referred to the facts that the sultan had died and that a customary payment was due his successor. The President responded to the Senate in a message dated February 22, in which he said he would act "in conformity with your resolution of advice" as soon as the necessary moneys were appropriated and ready.[94] By a special appropriations act of March 3, 1791, Congress appropriated $20,000 for the Moroccan treaty.[95] No further steps were taken concerning a naval force or the Algiers prisoners, however.[96]

This first set of interactions between the executive branch and Congress was marked by a straightforward, detailed, and, on the whole, complete executive branch account to the Congress of the state of affairs.[97] It illustrated the President's inclination to wait for congressional judgment as well as Jefferson's inclination to make recommendations. No doubt was entertained about the ultimate authority of the Congress. Furthermore, both branches displayed a consensus that at times the interests of the country demanded secrecy. Perhaps the most important aspect is that at the outset the executive branch, because any solution depended on appropriations, recognized the need to deal with Congress as a whole. This last matter became controversial in the spring of 1792.

The previous December, Jefferson had forwarded new information to the Senate that suggested that accession of a new dey in Algiers provided a favorable moment for making a permanent arrangement with the regency. Also, Captain O'Brien urged, after six years of captivity, that something be done "to finally extricate your fourteen unfortunate subjects from their present state of bondage and adversity."[98] Of the twenty-one original captives, some had died and one had been privately ransomed. A Senate committee recommended a treaty.[99]

On March 11, 1792, in preparation for a meeting between the President and senators the next day, Washington and Jefferson discussed whether the President could proceed with treaty negotiations only with Senate authorization. These are Jefferson's notes on his consultation with the President:

My opinions run on the following heads:

We must go to Algiers with the cash in our hands. Where shall we get it? By loan? By converting money now in the treasury?

Probably a loan might be obtained on the President's authority; but as this could not be repaid without a subsequent act of legislature, the Representatives might refuse it.

So if [we] convert money in [the] treasury, they may refuse to sanction it.

The subsequent approbation of the Senate being necessary to validate a treaty[,] they expect to be consulted beforehand if the case admits.

So the subsequent act of the Representatives being necessary where money is given, why should not they expect to be consulted in like manner when the case admits. A treaty is a law of the land. But prudence will point out this difference to be attended to in making them; viz. where a treaty contains such articles only as will go into execution of themselves, or be carried into execution by the judges, they may be safely made; but where there are articles which require a law to be passed afterwards by the legislature, great caution is requisite.

[E].g., the consular convention with France required a very small legislative regulation. This convention was unanimously ratified by the Senate. Yet the same identical men threw by the law to enforce it at the last session, & the Representatives at this session have placed it among the laws which they may take up or not at their own convenience, as if that was a higher motive than the public faith.

Therefore against hazarding this transaction without the sanction of both Houses.

The President concurred. The Senate express[ed] the motive for this proposition, to be a fear that the Representatives would not keep the secret. He has no opinion of the secrecy of the Senate.[100]

Apparently Washington met with strong resistance from the senators, as is evidenced by Jefferson's notes from April 9:

The President had wished to redeem our captives at Algiers, & to make peace with them on paying an annual tribute. The Senate were willing to approve this, but unwilling to have the lower House applied to previously to furnish the money; they wished the President to take the money from the treasury, or open a loan for it. They thought that to consult the Representatives on one occasion, would give them a handle always to claim it, & would let them into a participation of the power of making treaties, which the constitution had given exclusively to the President & Senate. They said too, that if the particular sum was voted by the Representatives, it would not be a secret. The President had no confidence in the secresy of the Senate, & did not chuse to take money from the treasury or to borrow. But he agreed he would enter into provisional treaties with the Algerines, not to be binding on us till ratified here. I prepared questions for consultation with the Senate, and added, that the Senate were to be apprized that on the return of the provisional treaty, & after they should advise the ratification, he would not have the seal put to it till the *two* Houses should vote the money. He asked me if the treaty stipulating a sum & ratified by him, with the advice of the Senate, would not be good under the constitution, & obligatory on the Representatives to furnish the money? I answered it certainly would, & that it would be the duty of the representatives to raise the money; but that they might decline to do what was their duty, & I thot it might be incautious to commit himself by a ratification with a foreign nation, where he might be left in the lurch in the execution: it was possible too, to conceive a treaty, which it would not be their duty to provide for. He said that he did not like throwing too much into democratic hands, that if they would not do what the constitution called on them to do, the government would be at an end, and must *then assume another form.* He stopped here; & I kept silence to see whether he would say anything more in the same line, or add any qualifying expression to soften what he had said, but he did neither.[101]

Washington had obviously come to the conclusion that a negotiated redemption of the American prisoners was the only realistic option. Washington and Jefferson also believed that realism, if not constitutional necessity, made it highly desirable to have the House approve of the negotiations beforehand. Washington was not about to borrow the necessary money on his own authority. The Senate insisted on having a special role and brought the need for secrecy into play, although the President was not impressed by the Senate's allegedly superior capacity to keep secrets. Following behind-the-scenes discussions, all of these considerations were brought into finely tuned balance when, on a single day, May 8, 1792, the President formally asked the Senate whether it would approve both ransom and a treaty and, if so, at what price. The Senate advised the President that a peace treaty with Algiers not to exceed $40,000, plus subsequent annual tribute not to exceed $25,000, plus ransom not to exceed $40,000, would be approved.[102] Finally, the Congress made a special appropriation of $50,000 "to defray any expense which might be incurred in relation to the intercourse between the United States and foreign nations."[103] The purpose of this last appropriation was understood to be money for Algiers, but in order to protect the negotiations this intention was not publicly stated.

Fearing interference from foreign countries, especially England, which was widely thought to be hostile to American interests and competition, the next steps were taken in extreme secrecy. Washington, Jefferson, and Thomas Pinckney, the new American minister to London, were the only ones to know of the President's appointments of Admiral John Paul Jones, then in London, as commissioner for negotiations with Algiers, and of Thomas Barclay, the U.S. consul at Morocco, as his substitute should Jones not be available. Detailed instructions were issued for the negotiations.[104]

When Pinckney arrived in London, he learned of Jones's death. Barclay received the papers and prepared to depart for Algiers, but he became ill and died in Lisbon in January 1793. At the end of March, Washington appointed the American minister to Portugal, David Humphreys, as commissioner. At this point the strategic situation deteriorated considerably. At the beginning of October 1793, in Gibraltar, Humphreys learned that the much-dreaded truce between Algiers and Portugal had been concluded and that Algerine corsairs were on their way to the Atlantic. The negotiations had been carried out by William Logie, the British consul in Algiers, on behalf of Portugal, although not necessarily with Portugal's informed consent. Edward Church, the U.S. consul in Lisbon, concluded that England was responsible: "The conduct of the British in this business leaves no room to doubt or mistake their object, which was evidently aimed at us . . . As a further confirmation, it is worthy of remark, that the same British agent obtained a truce at the same time between the States of Holland and the Dey, for six months, whereby we and the Hanse Towns are now left the only prey to those barbarians."[105]

On December 16 the President presented to both Houses of Congress a report from the Secretary of State that contained much of the diplomatic correspondence. Washington requested secrecy:

While it is proper our citizens should know that subjects which so much concern their interests and their feelings, have duly engaged the attention of their Legislature and Executive, it would still be improper that some particulars of this communication should be made known. The confidential conversation stated in one of the last letters sent herewith is one of these. Both justice and policy require that the source of that information should remain secret. So a knowledge of the sums meant to have been given for peace and ransom might have a disadvantageous influence on future proceedings for the same objects.[106]

In connection with the House debates on the President's message, secrecy became controversial, and the House amended its standing order in favor of House discretion. The issue had acquired partisan overtones, with Republicans arguing for the amendment. This was also the time of heated controversy over the Neutrality Proclamation, the alliance with France, and relations with Great Britain. Nevertheless, after adoption of the amendment, the House defeated by a one-vote margin a motion to go into public session on Algiers.[107] Indeed, on January 2, 1794, the House adopted secret resolutions authorizing additional money for the negotiations and calling for a naval force "adequate to the protection of the commerce of the United States against the Algerine corsairs."[108] On January 7 the House lifted the injunction of secrecy concerning these resolutions and requested a committee to edit the President's communication in accord with his suggestions. That task was accomplished by February 6.[109]

While Congress was considering possible responses to the changed circumstances, the administration received new information that made matters even worse. The President forwarded this information, on a confidential basis, on March 3, 1794.[110] During October and November Algiers had captured eleven American vessels and 105 American seamen in the Atlantic, and the dey had firmly refused any negotiations with the United States.[111] Congress was bombarded with petitions not only from the hostages, but also from merchants calling for adequate naval protection.[112] Insurance rates on American shipping increased from 10 to 30 percent.[113]

In a letter to Humphreys, Pierre Eric Skjoldebrand, brother of the Swedish consul in Algiers and an informal American agent, held out some hope that if the dey could be talked to in a "favorable" moment, matters might be settled.[114] Apparently on this basis, it was decided that Congress should make further efforts for a negotiated peace providing realistic amounts of ransom and naval armament.

Since 1790 Congress had made $40,000 available annually for "intercourse between the United States and foreign nations," and had given the President discretion not to account specifically for expenditures that he thought it inadvisable to make public.[115] The latter procedure was regularized in 1793 by a formal system of certificates that were deemed to be a "sufficient voucher."[116] On March 20, 1794, Congress appropriated $1 million in addition to all previous appropriations "to defray any expenses which may be incurred, in relation to the intercourse between the United States and foreign nations." The legislation included authority to borrow the amount needed and called for an account of the expenditures "as soon as may be."[117] That it was almost half as much as regular 1794 appropriations for the support of the government and the military establishment gives a sense of the magnitude of this appropriation for a vaguely stated purpose.[118]

A naval bill called for additional moneys. Almost three months after he had left the office of Secretary of State, Jefferson, in a limited way, got what he had requested three years earlier, and what he would use during his own Presidency—a naval force to deal with the Barbary Powers. The proposal was, on the whole, not very popular in the House. Madison opposed it, arguing that it would be cheaper to purchase peace.[119] If the British were behind Algiers, as was widely assumed though not proven, then the existence of such a fleet would increase the danger of war with England.[120] Madison thus attempted to undercut the Federalists, who favored the naval bill, by linking the Algiers issue to the greater dispute over relations with England and France.[121] The House nevertheless approved the bill by an eleven-vote majority. The act of March 27, 1794, authorized six ships, but also provided that the program should be dropped if "a peace shall take place between the United States and the Regency of Algiers."[122] Congress assigned priority to the negotiations.

The President took immediate steps to implement the legislation.[123] When a peace treaty with Algiers was eventually concluded, Congress reduced the shipbuilding program to three frigates, which were launched in 1797.[124] The entire expense for building, arming, and keeping the ships in commission for the years 1794–1798 was about $2.5 million. Ray W. Irwin has argued that the great expense was, however, dwarfed by the savings in insurance premiums following the launching of the frigates.[125]

After considerable further difficulties, Humphreys' agent for these negotiations, Joseph Donaldson, agreed to a treaty at the end of 1795. Humphreys approved the treaty, "reserving the same, nevertheless, for the final ratification of the President of the United States of America, by and with the advice and consent of the Senate."[126] The terms had used up more money than Congress had appropriated and included maritime and military stores; in short, it was "cash and arms for hostages."[127]

The President submitted the treaty to the Senate on February 15, 1796, with much of the diplomatic correspondence.[128] It was promptly ratified. When efforts to secure the necessary gold and silver in the war-torn European markets caused delays, the dey announced that he would declare war on the United States—the threat caused a thirty-six-gun frigate for "the Dey's daughter" to be added to the previous expenses.[129] On May 30, 1796, Congress appropriated an additional $260,000 for treaties with the Barbary Powers.[130] The surviving American hostages were released in June 1796, some after eleven years of captivity.

The episode came to an end on February 22, 1797, when the House voted further appropriations of approximately $350,000,[131] for a total of Algiers expenditures in excess of $1.5 million. In opening the session of Congress, Washington had said: "After many delays and disappointments, arising out of the European war, the final arrangements for the fulfilling of the engagements made to the Dey and Regency of Algiers, will, in all present appearance, be crowned with success, but under great, though inevitable disadvantages in the pecuniary transactions, occasioned by that war, which will render a further provision necessary."[132] The House resolved first to call for an accounting.[133] The President responded within a week, submitting to both Houses, "in confidence," detailed reports from the secretaries of State and Treasury. On February 21, 1797, the House, after a secret debate on the appropriations, voted overwhelmingly that the injunction of secrecy imposed on the report be lifted and "that all future debates and proceedings thereon be had with open doors."[134] However, it exempted from publication an important letter detailing the matters of the additional frigate and payments made to various Algerine officials and an Algerine banker who had served as a go-between and financial broker.[135]

The United States' first encounter with hostage-taking had ended. The plight of the captives, merchant pressure, lack of a navy, geographic distance, and the European wars had forced the United States to behave in the same manner in which many, more important, European powers had behaved for a long time. When Jefferson, as President, faced the problem anew after the bashaw of Tripoli declared war in 1801, he sent the Navy.[136] He justified his action as a training exercise, invoking an act of Congress passed during the last session of the Adams administration providing for a "Naval Peace Establishment."[137] Sending the Navy helped to some extent. The bashaw, following the grounding of the frigate *Philadelphia* in October 1803, captured more than 300 American seamen, for whom the United States, as the result of a peace treaty in 1805, paid only $60,000 in ransom. That amount was much less than the $3 million originally demanded by the bashaw or the amount that had been paid to Algiers.

Relations with Algiers began to sour again in 1812. New hostages were taken. On February 23, 1815, Madison asked Congress for a declaration of war.[138] Congress responded on March 3, not with a formal declaration of war, but with legislation authorizing the President to employ "such of the armed vessels of the United States as may be judged requisite."[139] This time it was the United States' turn to dictate a peace treaty to the dey on "unprecedented" terms.[140] When the dey reneged on that treaty, President Madison, in his annual message on December 3, 1816, advised Congress that he would use naval force if necessary.[141] The United States compelled the dey, on December 23, to sign yet another treaty.[142] However, given that the European powers had also become unwilling to put up with Barbary piracy, the treaty had become more or less irrelevant. In fact it was forgotten in the State Department and was not submitted by President Monroe for Senate ratification until December 1821.[143] In 1830 Algiers became part of the French colonial empire.

Because it did not generate the same partisan passions as the Neutrality Proclamation or the Jay Treaty, the Algiers episode is far less well known than other foreign policy issues of the Washington administration and has been largely ignored. The difficulties that it posed, however, were great and intractable. Precisely because it was relatively free of partisanship, it framed the questions concerning the distribution of powers in a more detached manner. In any event, Washington's actions surrounding his unilateral proclamation of "neutrality" after France had declared war against England in 1793, and the Jay Treaty with England, concluded in 1795, displayed, by and large, the same constitutional circumspection that characterized his administration's conduct with respect to the Barbary Powers.[144]

The Constitution does not speak in such abstractions as the foreign affairs power or the war power. Nor, as the Washington administration addressed the Algiers problem, were these two powers thought of as meaningful. When Jefferson told Congress in 1790 that it had to decide "between war, tribute, and ransom," he said about the latter two that Congress had the duty to limit and provide the amount, and the executive had the duty "to make arrangements for employing it to the best advantage."[145] In context, this meant that negotiations and treaty drafts were the task of the executive department, but that Congress shared responsibility and control through its power of the purse, and the Senate through its treaty power.

As to Algiers, Washington sought advice, and advice was rendered by the Senate, which set limits on the amount of ransom it would accept as the result of negotiations. Although one may safely assume that informal discussions lay behind formal messages and resolutions, the administration did not proceed with negotiations without formal authority contained in Senate resolutions or congressional appropriations. The instructions the administration unilaterally chose to give the commissioners were carefully framed in accordance with the stipulated monetary limitations.[146] To the extent that they were exceeded, it was due to the necessities faced by the negotiators. If Congress remained in the dark, so did the executive due to the unsatisfactory communications system of the period. However, the Senate's treaty functions were formally preserved by the appropriate treaty stipulations.

The Washington administration did not always follow as strict a course of consultations as it did during the Algiers business.[147] It was quite conscious of the fact that occasionally the secrecy of diplomatic overtures was the condition of success. On the other hand, the extent to which, in general, the administration disclosed details of foreign negotiations to the Congress and to the public at large was remarkable and, indeed, worried some political observers.[148] Frequently Washington informed Congress by literally taking it into "his confidence." This mode of interaction was subject to two limitations. On the one hand, the executive branch claimed the right to withhold information if even its limited publication would be against public interest. On the other hand, the House eventually claimed the right to lift injunctions of secrecy. Whether the practices of the government with respect to secrecy ran counter to the spirit of the framers' plan and the demands of popular sovereignty is a difficult question.[149] Washington displayed awareness of these demands but was also troubled by "throwing too much into democratic hands."[150] On the whole, however, the administration seemed to be determined to achieve the highest possible degree of coordination for American policy toward Algiers, and not only kept Congress informed, but actually consulted it beforehand.

With regard to the respective powers of the Senate and the House, the administration's approach in the Algiers matter was arguably at some variance with the President's position in the Jay Treaty controversy. Discussing Algiers with his Secretary of State, Washington had raised the question of whether the House was under a constitutional obligation to furnish moneys stipulated in a ratified treaty. Jefferson responded that the House "certainly" had such an obligation, but then equivocated by conceiving of hypothetical treaties "which it would not be their duty to provide for."[151]

In the summer of 1795, following the Senate's approval, with some modification, of the Jay Treaty, Washington asked the House to provide $90,000 to pay for arbitral commissions established by the treaty. This action led to an intense dispute about the House's power to demand the instructions and other documents relating to the treaty. The very partisan debate had a somewhat "academic" character because the Senate had received all the papers, and the House members apparently could inspect them at the Senate.[152] The House overwhelmingly adopted a resolution calling for the papers, excepting only those "as any existing negotiation may render improper to be disclosed."[153]

Washington refused, invoking the needs of foreign negotiations and the constitutional separation of powers that gave the House no role in the treaty-making process: "[It] is essential to the due administration of the Government, that the boundaries fixed by the Constitution between the different departments should be preserved." Earlier in his message, Washington indicated that the situation would be different if the House contemplated impeachment. He also stressed that he had "no disposition to withhold any information which the duty of my station will permit, or the public good shall require, to be disclosed."[154] This latter language could, of course, cover the full disclosures made in connection with the Algiers negotiations.

Jefferson, then at Monticello, seems to have remained on the sidelines of this dispute, although he did tell Madison about the position he had taken favoring inclusion of both branches of the legislature in the Algiers arrangements.[155] Dumas Malone, Jefferson's biographer, however, has found no evidence suggesting that Jefferson had anything to do with Virginia's proposed constitutional amendment that aimed at formalizing participation of the House in the treaty process when the subject matter of a treaty concerned congressional powers.[156]

Although the strong views that Washington expressed on this occasion had already been foreshadowed vaguely in his exchange with Jefferson at the beginning of the Algiers episode, his conduct in the course of that drawn-out business is well summarized by his own characterization of his overall attitude in the message rejecting the House request for the Jay Treaty papers: "[I]t has been, as it will continue to be, while I have the honor to preside in the Government, my constant endeavor to harmonize with the other branches thereof, so far as the trust delegated to me by the people of the United States, and my sense of the obligation it imposes, to 'preserve, protect, and defend the Constitution,' will permit."[157]

"A More Effectual Mode of Administering"

The shaping of governmental structures began in earnest in 1789 and, of course, has continued ever since. Precedents were set by the President and Congress in response to complex problems as they occurred, and were influenced by earnest considerations of principles and practical considerations of statecraft, but also, to be sure, by political considerations.[158] The process was helped initially by the relative absence of partisanship. It was also helped by the circumspection of Washington, who has found few matches among later Presidents in the deliberateness with which he worried about what was right for the government as a whole, without concentrating unduly on the powers of the presidency.

Such matters as the structure and accountability of executive departments were handled with discretion and common sense. The fact that Congress in general, and the House of Representatives in particular, had the ultimate word on financial matters led to coordination even in the area of foreign policy, at least where this seemed most necessary. The House, on the other hand, though not recognizing an "executive privilege" as such, was sensitive to the needs of confidentiality in the conduct of foreign policy. The investigatory powers of the House were taken seriously by the executive branch. The "advisory" functions of the Senate as to appointments and treaties posed an intricate problem that Washington tried to solve as well as he could—though without much success, given the awkwardness inherent in the involvement of a legislative chamber and the exigencies of foreign negotiations. Although the special responsibility of the President for the maintenance of foreign relations was understood, neither the President nor the Congress assumed that the executive had what John Locke, in his version of separation of powers, called the "federative" power, which pertained to foreign relations and which Locke classified as an executive power.[159]

Madison stated, in *The Federalist No. 45,* that the change brought about by the new Constitution was much less the addition of new powers to the union than the invigoration of its original powers: "The proposed change does not enlarge these powers; it only substitutes a more effectual mode of administering them."[160] To some extent this statement may have been no more than an argument to help make the new Constitution more acceptable. One should remember, on the other hand, that Madison was disappointed by the outcome of the Constitutional Convention and thought that the changes made were too modest.[161] In any event, what is more striking about the issues under review here is how much the concern of all participants was "an effectual mode of administering" the powers of the federal government. The main reference point for this concern was the constitutional framework rather than procrustean theories. Separation of powers notions played a supportive role, but the views expressed were not doctrinaire—in part because there was no clear doctrine. In general, little single-mindedness existed. What the New Hampshire constitution, in its separation of powers provision, had referred to as "the chain of connection that binds the whole fabric of the constitution" was perceived, if at times only dimly and without the "amity" that New Hampshire had postulated.[162]

3

APPROPRIATIONS
OF POWER

In this chapter I turn to the mundane subject of money. As the following pages make clear, though, there is much that is heroic in the mundane.

The appropriations clause of Article I, Section 7—"No money shall be drawn from the Treasury but in consequence of appropriations made by law"—is neither self-defining nor self-executing.[1] Nevertheless, few doubt the function of the clause as a prophylactic provision that reinforces the Constitution's version of separation of powers by thwarting potential claims of inherent power: the fact that there is a surplus in the Treasury and a good reason, even a reason authorized by law, to spend the money does not empower the executive branch to "draw from the Treasury."[2] Legislative control of money is well-nigh absolute. If it goes uncontrolled, it does so only because the legislature itself is out of control.

Historical Roots in English Appropriations Law

It took the English constitution many centuries of advances and retreats to establish the principle if not the form of legislative supremacy. As Frederic William Maitland noted: "throughout the Middle Ages the king's revenue had been in a very true sense the king's revenue, and parliament had but seldom attempted to give him orders as to what he should do with it."[3] As late as 1765 William Blackstone still distinguished between the king's "ordinary" and "extraordinary" revenue. The former was "the proper patrimony of the crown," while the latter was the supplies granted "by the commons of Great Britain, in parliament assembled." By the time of Blackstone the "extraordinary" grants had, however, become the ordinary source of revenue for the royal household and the operations of the government. Blackstone viewed this development as fortunate "for the liberty of the subject."[4]

Extraordinary needs of the crown in times of war led to the refinement of appropriations law. Two statutes enacted within a short period during the reign of Charles II illustrate the development in capsule form. At the beginning of the second of the Dutch Wars, Parliament granted a "royal aid" in the amount of nearly 2.5 million pounds: the amount to be "raised, leavyed and paid unto your Majestie" within a period of three years. The preamble of the "Act for Granting Royall Ayd" conceptualized the grant as a reimbursement for "vast expenses" incurred by Charles II in preparation for war. The Crown had done what was necessary, and the grateful Commons did what was fair.[5]

When the war continued (Louis XIV joined the Dutch side in January 1666), the effort required considerably more money. Parliament levied a new tax but this time provided for the segregation of these funds as they came into and went out of the Exchequer. The "Act for Raising Moneys by a Toll and otherwise toward the Maintenance of the present Warr" prohibited the spending of these revenues other than by warrant mentioning that "the Moneyes payable . . . are for the service of Your Majestie in the said Warr respectively."[6] Parliament did what was necessary and made sure that the Crown would do what was fair.

According to Maitland this precedent was not followed by the Parliament of James II, but it generated the rule after the Glorious Revolution. As John Brewer summarizes, "the reign of James II had demonstrated that disastrous and divisive policies could easily be pursued by a monarch unconstrained by the need to consult 'the representatives of the people.' " A member of Parliament from the period formulated the crucial insight, "'tis money that makes a Parliament considerable & nothing else."[7]

Parliament displayed the new rigor in appropriations even before enactment of the English Bill of Rights in 1689—symbolically suggesting Blackstone's point that there was a relation to the "liberty of the subject." An elaborate act that was passed at the very beginning of the reign of William and Mary levied a tax and appropriated the first 400,000 pounds to be collected for the service of the navy. The statute broke down this amount further into expenditure categories of 100,000 pounds each. The statute said expressly that the sum appropriated to these uses "may not be diverted or applyed to any other Purpose" and required a separate account, specific warrants, and forfeiture of the like amount on the part of those who might divert any of these funds.[8] After 1691 Parliament supplemented the 1688 statute with so-called Commissions of Public Accounts for the purpose of scrutinizing government revenue and expenditure.[9]

The Glorious Revolution confirmed the principle that Parliament controlled not only the raising of revenues by means of taxation but also the expenditure of these moneys. As one turns to ask what the implications of this approach might have been for the governance of the North American colonies, one must first of all keep in mind that what—after 1787—we have come to call "dual sovereignty" de facto prevailed even before the Revolution. The American colonists actually lived under two governments: the government in London and that of their colony, which, though not in possession of complete authority, managed "internal police" and levied taxes for local purposes.[10] Purposes for which taxes were levied were fairly limited. As Edwin Perkins has stressed, in normal years, salaries for the appointed governor, for a few judges, and in some provinces for the recognized clergy, plus compensation for their own legislative expenses, were typically major items in the annual budget.[11] One of the means employed to keep a firm grasp over government officials was to limit appropriations for these purposes to one year's duration and to distinguish between authorizations to spend money and actual spending bills. In addition, colonial legislatures developed ways to control disbursements and to audit accounts. Indeed, some elected their own treasurers to reduce executive influence.[12]

There were, of course, expenditures for purposes other than what in England had become identified as the "civil list." The creation of paper currency (under legislative control) often financed military campaigns against the French, the Spanish, and the Indians. In part the colonists undertook this debt in the hope that Parliament would eventually reimburse them for a substantial share of these expenses. When toward the end of the colonial period the king's ministers adopted new policies designed to shift more of the tax burden for defending North America and the Atlantic shipping lanes to the colonies themselves and to restrict, and perhaps even outlaw, the use of paper money, the War of Independence broke out.[13]

Fiscal Constitutions

As the newly independent states began the enterprise of constitution-making, there could be little doubt that they would base the new constitutions on the separation of powers doctrine (although opinions on what that entailed differed widely). There could also be little doubt that the new constitutions would continue and further strengthen the basic features of the fiscal constitution that had emerged in England and in the colonies.[14] The unquestioned rule was that of legislative supremacy.

The rule was unquestioned, though in the postrevolutionary American context not necessarily obvious. The rule had developed under the conditions of mixed government, in which king, aristocracy, and commons were differently based powers with different interests, including different economic interests. As we have seen, after the Declaration of Independence the issue was the separation of power flowing from a singular source—namely, the people. Yet, in the eyes of many, the fact that legislature and executive derived their legitimacy from the same source did not dispose of the ever-present danger of waste and corruption. As Herbert Storing has said: "Through limited grants of power, tight responsibility, and internal checks, the few may be prevented from doing much harm."[15] In other words, even after the Revolution, appropriations were seen as appropriations of power.

The fiscal provisions of the new state constitutions adopted from 1776 through 1787 differed, of course, from state to state and, in most instances, were surprisingly rudimentary.[16] We may attribute this rudimentary character mostly to the fact that essential elements had been worked out during the colonial period, and their basic soundness was not questioned. As to the mechanisms for controlling expenditures, many of the constitutions contained an origination clause of the kind that is also found, for revenue measures, in Article I, Section 7 of the U.S. Constitution and that in English constitutional history dates back as far as the beginning of the fifteenth century. "Money bills" were to originate in the more popular of the legislative chambers. One can find this approach, which was meant to assure that the frugality and economic interests of the common people were given their proper weight, in most of the new constitutions, although only New Jersey, South Carolina, and Virginia continued the roughly 100-year-old English rule of prohibiting upper house amendments to such bills.[17]

Second, the legislature usually "appointed" the treasurer or treasurers. The Maryland constitution reserved this power to the lower house.[18] And in fact the various drafts of the federal Constitution provided for appointment of the treasurer by joint ballot of both houses as late as September 14, 1787, when, in the interest of conformity, this appointment was subjected to the general approach of presidential nomination and Senate advice and consent.

Third, as to the matter of appropriations more specifically, only the constitutions of Maryland and Pennsylvania used the very word. Section 20 of the 1776 Pennsylvania constitution gave the Supreme Executive Council the power to "draw upon the treasury for such sums as shall be appropriated by the house."[19] Article 16 of the South Carolina constitution employed negative phrasing to the same effect, as did the U.S. Constitution a decade later. South Carolina ordained that "no money shall be drawn out of the public treasury but by the legislative authority of the State."[20] Other constitutions subjected gubernatorial spending to a warrant requirement. Still others were silent on the matter.

Fourth, the Maryland constitution of 1776 alone imposed procedural rules to limit trade-offs between fiscal and other policies. Article XI of the Maryland Constitution contained an admissibility rule of the kind that interests modern public choice theorists:

the House of Delegates shall not, on any occasion, or under any pretence, annex to, or blend with a money bill, any matter, clause, or thing, not immediately relating to, and necessary for the imposing, assessing, levying, or applying the taxes or supplies, to be raised for the support of the government, or the current expenses of the State: . . . every bill, assessing, levying, or applying taxes or supplies, for the support of government, or the current expenses of the State, or appropriating money in the treasury, shall be deemed a money bill.[21]

This "germaneness" requirement displays a high degree of sophistication concerning opportunities for manipulation of the legislative process. Among the original states only Massachusetts and New York recognized an overridable veto.

On the whole, the fiscal provisions of the state constitutions confirm our understanding that during the founding period money matters were thought of primarily as a legislative prerogative. The reason for this was not simply the insight that appropriations were appropriations of power. It was also the—for us perhaps counterintuitive—hope that assuring legislative supremacy in fiscal matters would bring about the moderation, temperance, and frugality without which free government would be endangered.[22] The New Hampshire Bill of Rights of 1784, in a limitation on the appropriations power, referred to "economy" as "a most essential virtue in all states."[23] James McHenry, a delegate to the Constitutional Convention from Maryland and in the last years of the eighteenth century Washington's and Adams' Secretary of War, neatly summarized these considerations. McHenry explained the appropriations clause of the federal Constitution to the Maryland House of Delegates in November 1787: "When the Public Money is lodged in its Treasury there can be no regulation more consistant with the Spirit of Economy and free Government that it shall only be drawn forth under appropriation by Law and this part of the proposed Constitution could meet with no opposition as the People who give their Money ought to know in what manner it is expended."[24]

Organization and control of "the public's treasury" had been among the most contested issues in the congress of state delegates that served as the central lawmaking and governing institution of the Confederation.[25] In Philadelphia these matters remained essentially unresolved. It was left to the First Congress to determine the exact structure of the Treasury. As we saw in the previous chapter, the legislation establishing the Department of the Treasury placed the department in a class by itself. Unlike the acts concerning the departments of State and War, it did not refer to the Treasury as an "executive" department even though the secretary was removable by the President. It also spelled out in detail an elaborate set of officers. In contrast to the other two statutes, the Treasury legislation was silent as to a presidential power of directing the secretary. Section 2 of the legislation listed, among the duties of the secretary, "to prepare and report estimates of public revenue, and the public expenditures" and "to grant under the limitations herein established, or to be hereafter provided, all warrants for monies to be issued from the Treasury, in pursuance of appropriations by law."[26]

The Congress saw the Secretary of the Treasury as an

indispensable, direct arm of the House in regard to its responsibilities for revenues and appropriations. The arrangements reflected the incapacity of the House in the spring and summer of 1789 to come to grips with the questions of what expenditures (especially in relation to the war debt) would be necessary and what revenues might be available. The House had appointed a committee to look into these matters as early as April of that year.[27] When its report raised more questions than it answered, a committee referred to as a "Committee of Ways and Means" took its place "to consider the report of a committee appointed to prepare an estimate of supplies requisite for the services of the United States for the current year, and to report thereon."[28] This second committee was discharged and its business referred to the Secretary of the Treasury as soon as the latter had been appointed.[29] The House ordered that "the Secretary of the Treasury do report to this House an estimate of the sums requisite to be appropriated during the present session of Congress, towards defraying the expenses of the Civil List, and of the Department of War, to the end of the present year."[30]

The First Appropriations Bills

Alexander Hamilton was more than ready. Within days of his appointment, he reported a detailed estimate accompanied by four schedules covering everything, including the prorated salaries of various doorkeepers.[31] The appropriations act that followed on September 29 essentially adopted Hamilton's estimates and aggregated expenditures into the four categories he had employed. The first act "making Appropriations for the Service of the present year" consisted of one single section and read as follows:

That there be appropriated for the service of the present year, to be paid out of the monies which arise, either from the requisitions heretofore made upon the several states, or from the duties on impost and tonnage, the following sums, viz. A sum not exceeding two hundred and sixteen thousand dollars for defraying the expenses of the civil list, under the late and present government; a sum not exceeding one hundred and thirty-seven thousand dollars for defraying the expenses of the department of war; a sum not exceeding one hundred and ninety thousand dollars for discharging warrants issued by the late board of treasury, and remaining unsatisfied; and a sum not exceeding ninety-six thousand dollars for paying the pensions to invalids.[32]

In separation of powers terms, these developments during the first session of the First Congress are of considerable moment. First of all, for purposes of developing estimates for appropriations, the House viewed the Treasury Secretary as its own agent. Second, while the supremacy of Congress was not in question, de facto only the executive branch developed and indeed had the capacity to digest and prepare the necessary information. As early as 1789 the basic pattern of interaction was established, with the secretary responsible for "estimates" of how much needed to be appropriated. Third, the first appropriations act continued to employ the concept of a "civil list" and distinguished from that civil list the expenditures necessary for the War Department—a matter of considerable consequence later on. Fourth, by aggregating expenditures into lump sums the act raised the important separation of powers question of what legal significance the underlying detail has. Finally, it brings to the fore the equally noteworthy question as to the significance for the operations of the government of the formula "a sum not exceeding."[33]

In January 1790, as part of his larger "Report relative to a Provision for the Support of Public Credit," Hamilton gave his estimates for the year 1790.[34] He submitted a supplementary report in early March.[35] The "Act making appropriations for the support of government for the year one thousand seven hundred and ninety," dated March 26, once again distinguished among civil list, War Department, and invalid pensioners and employed aggregate figures. This time, however, the legislation specifically incorporated the estimates. For instance, the act appropriated a sum not exceeding $141,492.73 "for defraying the expenses of the civil list, as estimated by the Secretary of the Treasury." Where estimates were beside the point, as in an appropriation of $10,000 for "contingencies of the government," the act asked the President to account for expenditures by the end of the year.[36]

The legislation also made clear that Congress ordinarily distinguished between authorizing legislation and appropriations by a separate provision authorizing the payment of various specified debts to individuals "not heretofore provided for by law, and estimated in the . . . report of the

Secretary."[37] This distinction had previously figured in the House debates when an attempt was made from the floor to reimburse lighthouse expenses for Charleston, South Carolina—an attempt rebuffed as "a bill of appropriations, and not of grants."[38] Porkbarrel had raised its ugly head: "Should this be granted, every member in this House will come foreward with proposals for clearing rivers, and opening canals to the source of rivers."[39]

The acerbic Senator William Maclay from Pennsylvania complained bitterly about the manner in which the 1790 appropriations act had been pushed through the Senate without his even being able to get a copy of the bill. Failing to appreciate that from his vantage point the bill actually represented a technical advance, he thought that the lump sum appropriations gave the secretary the money "for him to account for as he pleases."[40] In reality Congress had appropriated no such power. As Lucius Wilmerding points out, Hamilton, at the beginning of the month, had asked the House to provide rewards for the apprehension of counterfeiters: "The Secretary further begs leave to observe, that occasions occur from time to time, which fall under no stated head of expenditure, for which provision in some mode or other is necessary."[41] This is hardly the language of an executive branch considering itself free of constraints.

The 1791 appropriations act took essentially the same approach as that of the prior year.[42] By the end of 1791, however, attitudes began to change as the partisan tensions that had been generated by the controversy over the Bank of the United States lingered on and the Republicans began to emerge as a more or less organized faction led by Jefferson and Madison.[43] Hamilton conveyed his estimates for 1792 in November 1791. The total of a little more than $1 million included about $50,000 "to make good deficiencies" in prior estimates—an indication that the government had exceeded its authority.[44] Most items in the list of deficiencies pertain to expenditures authorized by law in 1791 but lacking appropriations. Deficiency appropriations in practice covered advances made in anticipation of appropriations.[45] Annual appropriations were frequently delayed until well after the new year. Indeed, as Hamilton pointed out after leaving office, Congress had made advances to its members "in anticipation of their respective compensations."[46]

The House debate on a committee bill for the 1792 appropriations led to a fair amount of acrimony over whether the committee should first have inquired into the expenditures under previous appropriations. James Madison considered "the present a good opportunity to determine how far the House could go into an examination of the accounts of public officers. It was true, that the Representatives of the people were the guardians of the public money, and consequently it was their duty to satisfy themselves as far as possible of the sources from which money flowed into the Treasury—how that money was applied—under what authority—and to inquire, at different times what balance remained in the Treasury."[47] As is so often the case, good republican principles resurfaced when they also served partisan purposes. Any attempt to understand the development of the appropriations process in the last decade of the eighteenth century must appreciate that it coincided with the emergence of parties.

The 1792 Appropriations Act was a rare example of one that became law before the beginning of the year to which it applied. Although in all important respects it followed Hamilton's estimates to a fraction of a penny, the statute appropriated aggregate amounts of money, followed by the formula "that is to say" and lists of expenditures that had either been lifted from Hamilton's "General Estimate for the Services of the Ensuing Year"[48] or adapted from his more detailed estimates. The language now ran along the following lines: for the service of the year and the support of the civil list, there shall be appropriated a sum of money not exceeding x dollars, "that is to say" for the compensation granted by law to the district judges so many dollars, for some other group of officials y dollars, for some third purpose z dollars.[49] Congress was incorporating the principle of appropriations specificity into the statutory text.

The following year Congress carried appropriations specificity one step further by eliminating the distinction between civil and military expenditures as separate heads and by reducing the dollar amounts attached to each specific item. When the original House bill reached the Senate, the Senate aggregated all War Department items into one sum. The subsequent House debate on the amended bill stressed separation of powers issues and is of great interest even though the reporter unfortunately provided only the most general summary. Some argued that the Senate approach left too much discretion to the department head, who "might apply the whole to a few of the objects . . . and leave all the other unsupported"; the argument suggests that there was doubt about the legal force of the underlying estimates.[50] The House defeated the Senate amendment by one vote, and, for 1793, the Senate yielded. The 1793 Appropriations Act contained one unwieldy appropriations section consisting of a single paragraph that covers almost three pages in the Statutes at Large.[51]

The House took no action on the proposal to lodge some discretionary power in the President to meet contingencies: "for instance, it may be found expedient to mount the militia . . . and therefore in some cases to apply the money, specifically appropriated for some of the objects which might upon trial be discovered unnecessary, to other objects of real utility."[52] This argument indicates some understanding of the need for executive discretion, though apparently predicated on the notion that without a specific grant of authority there might be no power to shift funds from one purpose to another, even in the military arena. After all, as President Jefferson asked about a decade later, "where is the rule of legal construction to be found which ascribes less effect to the words of an appropriation law, than of any other law?"[53]

Congress approved the appropriations act for 1793 on February 28 of that year. At the same time Jefferson and the Republicans pursued their full-fledged personal attack on Secretary Hamilton, who by now had become their favorite *bête noire,* suspected at all times of sinister schemes and purposes as he shuffled funds from one continent to another. The issue chosen involved two loans floated in Amsterdam and Antwerp on the basis of two acts of Congress. The charge was that Hamilton had intermingled these two loans although one had the purpose of servicing only the domestic debt of the United States and the other the purpose of paying the foreign debt.[54] Albert Gallatin, who in 1795 following his election to the House became the Republicans' financial expert, concluded in his 1796 *Sketch of the Finances of the United States* that the charge was "strictly and literally true," but "rather a want of form than a substantial violation of the appropriation law."[55] Hamilton, on the other hand, thought that he had had "considerable latitude of discretion" in "the business of the loans"[56] and justified himself in an astonishing number of reports produced "by virtue of demonic labor"[57] from February 4 through February 19, 1793.[58]

On February 27, Representative William Giles of Virginia, Jefferson's floor leader for this purpose, introduced nine resolutions of censure, all of which the House extensively debated the following two days and overwhelmingly defeated. The resolutions raise a host of fascinating separation of powers questions. I shall refer here only to the first of the resolutions, which read: "1. *Resolved* That it is essential to the due administration of the Government of the United States, that laws making specific appropriations of money should be strictly observed by the administrator of the finances thereof."[59] The ensuing debate was on the question whether this resolution should be sent to the Committee of the Whole House. The able William Loughton Smith, of South Carolina, opened the debate by saying that this late in the session was no time to discuss "theoretic principles of Government"; however, the future Federalist also argued: "Though the position contained in the first resolution, as a general rule, was not to be denied; yet it must be admitted, that there may be cases of sufficient urgency to justify a departure from it, and to make it the duty of the legislature to indemnify an officer."[60] Smith thus focused the controversy on what afterward became understood as a central question: should there only be one rigid rule or should exceptions to the rule be recognized?

The question grew into an exceedingly practical one the following year when the hypothetical about "mounting the militia" turned into a real case. In 1794 Congress did not enact annual appropriations before March. Civil and military appropriations were, for the first time, covered by two separate bills.[61] Both bills used the "that is to say" formula, although the one "making appropriations for the support of the military establishment of the United States" employed much more general categories than had been the case in 1793.

The legislation could not and did not foresee the most significant military expenditures of the year, created by Hamilton's and Washington's decision "to call forth" the militia against the Whiskey Rebellion.[62] On a provisional basis expenses were defrayed out of the money appropriated for the military establishment until Congress, after the fact, made the necessary appropriations.[63] In his *Sketch of the Finances* Gallatin took the position that this approach had been illegal: "The necessity of the measure may in the mind of the Executive have superseded every other consideration. The popularity of the Transaction may have thrown a veil over its illegality. But it should by no means be drawn hereafter as a precedent."[64]

Over the next six years, before he himself became the longest-serving Treasury Secretary in American History, Albert Gallatin played the role of the Republican gadfly stinging the Federalists. One of his purposes was the pursuit of economy.[65] Born and brought up in Geneva, he embodied that city's puritanism, plain living, and frugality.[66] His other purpose was to implement his views of separation of powers—views that were predicated on legislative supremacy in money matters.[67]

Gallatin's attempt to prevent any blending of powers employed several strategies. First, immediately upon taking his seat in the House, Gallatin saw to it that the chamber established a Committee on Ways and Means as he had known it in the Pennsylvania legislature.[68] Second, he fought for appropriations specificity by getting the Congress to amend the 1797 civil and military appropriations bills through tightening the statutory appropriations formula. It now read that for the expenditure of the civil list "the following sums be respectively appropriated; that is to say," and this formula was followed by the individual items without any aggregation. The appropriations act "for the military and naval establishments" was constructed according to the same model, except that it added the further stricture "which sums shall be solely applied to the objects for which they are respectively appropriated."[69] Gallatin said:

[H]is object in this amendment was, that each appropriation should be specific; that it might not be supposed to be in the power of the Treasury Department to appropriate to one object money which had been specifically appropriated for any other object. He did not know . . . whether, as to the Civil List, appropriations had ever been mixed, or whether it was understood that they might be so mixed; but they knew it had been officially declared that so far as related to the Military Department, the items had been totally mixed: for instance, if the estimate for clothing or any other item fell short, the officers of the Treasury did not think themselves bound by the particular appropriation, but had recourse to other items, for which larger sums were granted than there was occasion for. Such construction of the law . . . totally defeated the object of appropriation, and it was necessary therefore, so to express the law that no color for such a construction should be given.

Gallatin was concerned with what he saw as Federalist abuses and feared a "general relaxation" that placed the executive branch beyond the law.[70]

Although Gallatin won the 1797 battle, he lost the war for the remainder of the Federalist period. The 1798 and 1799 civil appropriations acts retained Gallatin's specificity formula.[71] For military appropriations, however, the Senate reverted to the old system. The 1798 act, which was not passed until June, made a lump-sum appropriation of $1.4 million; it introduced subcategories by using only the words "that is to say" and dropped the "shall be solely applied" stricture.[72] In light of the changes in legislative style that had been introduced in prior years, this reversion in language must be interpreted as a congressional ratification of executive branch discretion in military matters. For the years 1800 and 1801, the "respectively appropriated" language disappeared even from the civil appropriations.[73]

In separation of powers terms, there are two different ways of looking at these developments. On the one hand, they can be viewed as a battle over the power to disburse funds between legislative and executive elements that the executive won. While the governmental actors accepted the constitutional allocation of powers in the field of appropriations in principle, in practice they recognized exceptions that responded to the perceived need to anticipate appropriations and that gave the executive branch wide discretion in military appropriations.

On the other hand, and in my view more appropriately, these developments can be regarded as a continuing process of shaping governmental structures in the absence of clear and convincing customs. Considerations of principle and practical considerations of statecraft influenced Congress and the executive branch, as did considerations of political partisanship that increased as a confluence of ideological, economic, and organizational factors led to the emergence of identifiable political parties.

Partisanship furthered the "discovery" of appropriations specificity as a separation of powers concept. Yet appropriations specificity and its refinement through legislative drafting techniques also attempted to implement the rule of law in the area of government spending. One might indeed argue that the very return to prior legislative styles after 1797 reflected the acceptance rather than the rejection of the principle. By expressly choosing the old formula, Congress implicitly conferred discretion on the executive branch to shift funds from one head to another, at least in the military arena. The answer to Jefferson's rhetorical question—

"where is the rule of legal construction to be found which ascribes less effect to the words of an appropriation law, than of any other law?"—was that such rules of construction followed from the words employed by a knowing legislator who appropriated power in addition to money.

The spring of 1798, when partisan politics over France had reached a pitch and Congress had become unconstrained in spending on defense and foreign relations, opened other fronts where Gallatin could fight for legislative supremacy. His address of March 1, 1798, "in many respects the high point of Gallatin's legislative career,"[74] summed up his views on the role of appropriations in the constitutional separation of powers system. The argument had been advanced that Congress had an obligation to support financially the diplomatic establishment that the President thought was necessary. Gallatin answered:

This doctrine is as novel as it is absurd. We have always been taught to believe, that in all mixed Governments, and especially in our own, the different departments mutually operated as checks one upon the other. It is a principle incident to the very nature of those governments; it is a principle which flows from the distribution and separation of Legislative and Executive powers, by which the same act, in many instances, instead of belonging exclusively to either, falls under the discretionary and partial authority of both; it is a principle of all our state constitutions; it is a principle of the Constitution under which we now act . . . [A]lthough there is no clause which directs that Congress shall be bound to appropriate money in order to carry into effect any of the Executive powers, some gentlemen, recurring to metaphysical subtleties, and abandoning the literal and plain sense of the Constitution, say that . . . we . . . are under a moral obligation in this instance to grant the money. It is evident that where the Constitution has lodged the power, there exists the right of acting, and the right of discretion.

Gallatin's reference point was the constitutional framework, not some rigid theory: "The opinion of the Executive, and where he has a partial power, the application of that power to a certain object, will ever operate as powerful motives upon our deliberations. I wish it to have its full weight; but I feel averse to a doctrine which would place us under the sole control of a single force impelling us in a certain direction, to the exclusion of all the other motives of action which should also influence us."[75] These remarks represented more than a conciliatory gesture. Gallatin was neither obstinate nor impractical.

A few weeks after the March 1 speech, the House debated a $50,000 deficiency in the 1797 contingency expenditures of the Quartermaster's Department. Gallatin argued that the deficiency should not have been allowed to occur: "The Secretary of War was not justified in expending more in these contingencies than was appropriated, (except in case of necessity,) otherwise the Secretary of War, and not Congress, regulated the expenditure of money. It would be necessary to inquire into this business, and except some pressing necessity could be shown for going beyond the appropriation, he should consider the Secretary of War as highly blameable for having done so, as the appropriation is the only check which the Legislature has over the contingent expenses."[76] In short, in spite of the categorical nature of what he had to say about the "illegal" militia expenditures against the Whiskey Rebellion, Gallatin allowed for "pressing necessities." In this sense his view was not dramatically different from that of Hamilton, who in a 1799 letter to Secretary of War James McHenry commented that "disbursements finally must no doubt be regulated by the laws of appropriation. But provisory measures will often be unavoidable. And confidence must sometimes be reposed in after Legislative sanction and Provision . . . I would rather be responsible on proper occasions for formal deviations than for a feeble insufficient and unprosperous course of public business proceeding from an over-scrupulous adherence to general rules."[77]

If one gives due weight to the adjective "proper" in "on proper occasions," the main difference between Hamilton and Gallatin may lie in the adverb "often." Although Gallatin understood that a responsible official may sometimes have to act *ultra vires,* such acts were to be rare exceptions to the rule. He was not willing to develop a metatheory to account for exceptions, since otherwise the exceptions might swallow up the rule. He feared a "general relaxation."

The Heroic in the Mundane

This is the point at which we encounter the "heroic" dimensions of the mundane subject of money matters. Even in the business of appropriations it may, at times, be un-avoidable to make the sacrifice of risking one's career so that one may act "responsibly." In taking responsibility one cannot be sure of the concurrence of one's contemporaries, or the judgment of history. The Whiskey Rebellion pro-vides an illustration. As Gallatin suggested, the popularity of the transaction "may have thrown a veil over its illegal-ity."[78] In the court of history, however, the transaction has met with less approval. The judgment of at least one histo-rian differs substantially. To Jefferson's biographer, Dumas Malone, the armament "was represented by the govern-ment as a sign of the majesty of the law, and Hamilton's interpretation of it as a timely manifestation of the power of the young federal government was taken up by his parti-sans and afterwards commanded wide acceptance among historians. Since no opposition was encountered, this os-tentatious military display now appears disproportionate if not ridiculous."[79]

As we shall see fully in the next chapter, Thomas Jeffer-son, the President, and Albert Gallatin, the Treasury Secre-tary, deserve praise for not changing their views about the need for appropriations specificity once they switched sides and were in charge of the executive branch. Yet even Jeffer-son did not avoid heroism in the appropriations field. For example, when, in June 1807, the British ship *Leopard* at-tacked the American frigate *Chesapeake* in Hampton Roads to force the surrender of four seamen claimed to be British, the President had to start preparing for the worst. Four months later, on October 27, he sent a message to Congress in which he wrote as follows:

The moment our peace was threatened I deemed it indispensable to secure a greater provision of those military stores with which our magazines were not sufficiently furnished. To have awaited a previous and special sanction by law would have lost occasions which might not be retrieved. I did not hesitate, therefore, to authorize engagement for such supplements to our existing stock as would render it adequate to the emergencies threatening us, and I trust that the Legislature, feeling the same anxiety for the safety of our country . . . will approve, when done, what they would have seen so important to be done if then assembled.[80]

This fiscal heroism scarcely involved much risk for the President, as the *Chesapeake* incident had, according to Attorney General Caesar Augustus Rodney, "excited the spirit of 76 and the whole country is literally in arms."[81] Even so, when Congress gathered in October, John Randolph of Roanoke, by now a gadfly, "allowed that the crisis which occasioned the extraordinary expenses in question, was an imminent one. It was so critical, that Congress ought to have been immediately convened, in order that they might have given authority by law for these extraordinary expenses, and for adopting such measures, as national feeling and national honor called for."[82] Randolph went on, pressing his advantage rather ruthlessly:

He confessed he felt extremely reluctant to vote large sums for the support of our degraded and disgraced Navy, for expenses, too, that had been illegally incurred. He had endeavored in vain to procure Gallatin on Finance . . . In that book he recollected a case exactly opposite to the present, where the President of the United States during the Pennsylvania insurrection, made use of money to defray the expenses incurred, which had been appropriated for a different object; but not having the book in his possession he would not venture to quote it, lest he should not do it correctly.[83]

Randolph should have trusted his memory. But maybe his lawyer's point was beside the point. Had Jefferson done as Randolph thought he should have, who will doubt that Congress would have done what "national feeling and honor" called for? Maybe more, maybe too much. Maybe that is what Jefferson wanted to avoid. Maybe that is what was heroic about his failure to convene Congress. At the end of the debate in which Randolph was so critical of his erstwhile hero, a congressman from Pennsylvania by the name of John Smilie rose and invoked the example of an ancient nation "who were wont to discuss great national questions twice, once when they were drunk, that they might not want spirit, and once when they were sober, that they might not be deficient in prudence."[84] As our own experience continues to demonstrate, prudence in appropriations is perhaps the most desirable of all virtues in a legislator.

4

JEFFERSON'S
"SHACKLES OF POWER"

As we saw in the prior chapters, the Washington and Adams administrations forged precedents for the executive and legislative branches as they grappled with considerations of principle, statecraft, and politics. When Jefferson took office as President in 1801, the first phase of the formative era ended, and a second phase began, which might best be characterized as a testing phase. How much continuity and consistency would there be between prior practices and those of the new administration? Would the Jeffersonians in power adhere to the views expressed when in opposition? Further, how would Jefferson react to situations that tested the separation of powers but for which Washington and Adams had set no precedent? In his First Inaugural Address, when Jefferson acknowledged partisanship by denying it—"We are all Republicans, we are all Federalists"[1]—he glossed over the key question of how to separate the federal powers now that his party controlled both the President's

House and Capitol Hill. As in the decades of "divided government" since the Second World War, the meaning of
separation of powers differs with the changing nature of
congressional majorities.[2]

Indeed, Jefferson's own battle with the Federalist judiciary, the best known of separation of powers issues during
the Jefferson administration, illustrates how partisanship
invigorated the debate over separation of powers in the
formative era. The creation of separate circuit courts with
their own set of judges and the appointment of the "mid-
night judges" in the last days of the Adams administration
had led Jefferson to complain: "the Federalists have retired
into the Judiciary as a stronghold . . . and from that battery
all the works of republicanism are to be beaten down and
erased."[3] The separation of powers battle began with the
Republicans' repeal of the "Act to provide for the more
convenient organization of the Courts of the United
States,"[4] continued with the enhancement of judicial power
by Chief Justice Marshall in *Marbury v. Madison,* and included the unsuccessful effort on the part of Republicans to
convict the rambunctious Justice Samuel Chase of "high
crimes and misdemeanors" as well as the confrontation
between Marshall and Jefferson over executive prerogatives
during the Burr trial.[5]

The task of figuring out the appropriate role in a constitutional democracy for the third, allegedly "least dangerous," branch, was perhaps the most puzzling of all the
challenges the framers' generation faced. Yet in spite of all
the noise and clamor about overreaching judges, the judiciary remained the least consequential branch during the

early years of American government. In a way, former Chief Justice Jay was right when, in 1800, he declined reappointment as Chief Justice because he thought the bench lacked "energy, weight, and dignity."[6]

The relationship of Congress and the executive was a separation of powers issue of more immediate import. The "revolution of 1800"[7] was certainly not a revolution in the sense of a complete and pervasive change, but it did represent the first peaceful rotation of government in the history of the United States.[8] It opened a second phase in the formation of separation of powers practices, raising the twofold question of continuity with Federalist practices and consistency with views expressed by the Republicans before governmental responsibility became theirs.

Jefferson's Changing Roles: The Challenge of Consistency

On October 1, 1792, Secretary of State Thomas Jefferson paid a visit to President Washington at Mount Vernon. The two men were in a contemplative mood and talked about their future. Jefferson had previously written to Washington advising him of his desire to retire from public affairs. Washington himself said that he was disinclined to stand for a second term. He told Jefferson that "[n]obody disliked more the ceremonies of his office, and . . . [that] he had not the least taste or gratification in the execution of it's functions." For his part, the Secretary of State, not quite fifty years of age, was emphatic that he "ever preferred the pursuits of private life to those of public, which had nothing in them agreeable to [him]."[9] Public life seems, indeed, to have been so disagreeable to Jefferson that he is said to have suffered from "disabling headaches lasting two or three weeks that began when he first took public office and that disappeared only when he permanently retired from it."[10]

Assuming that Jefferson's negative attitude toward staying in the cabinet might have been influenced by the animosity that prevailed between the Secretary of State and the Secretary of the Treasury, Alexander Hamilton, especially concerning their differences over the sweep of executive power, the President stressed that he gave no credence to the idea that anybody wanted to transform the government into a monarchy. Jefferson, on the other hand, alleged that there was "a numerous sect" who contemplated monarchy and that Hamilton was one of them. Jefferson pointed to a "squadron" in Congress that was ready to do whatever the Secretary of the Treasury should direct. For his own part, Jefferson felt "[t]hat if the equilibrium of the three great bodies Legislative, Executive, & judiciary could be preserved, if the Legislature could be kept independant, I should never fear the result of such a government but that I could not but be uneasy when I saw that the Executive had swallowed up the legislative branch."[11]

Clearly, Jefferson favored legislative over executive power. Indeed, the hyperbole "revolution of 1800" refers to Jefferson's belief that he "had saved the country from monarchy and militarism, and brought it back to republican simplicity."[12] In the very first paragraph of his First Inaugural Address Jefferson addressed the members of Congress specifically: "To you, then, gentlemen, who are charged with the *sovereign* functions of legislation . . . I look with encouragement for that guidance and support which may enable us to steer with safety the vessel in which we are all embarked amidst the conflicting elements of a troubled world."[13]

Five years later, during Jefferson's second term as President, John Randolph, who had started out as the administration's leader in the House of Representatives but by now was an irreconcilable enemy, spoke against a resolution prohibiting the importation of British goods. "I have before protested, and I again protest against secret, irresponsible, overruling influence. The first question I asked when I saw the gentleman's resolution, was, 'Is this a measure of the Cabinet?' Not of an open declared Cabinet; but, of an invisible, inscrutable, unconstitutional Cabinet, without responsibility, unknown to the Constitution. I speak of back-stairs influence—of men who bring messages to this House, which, although they do not appear on the Journals, govern its decisions." Randolph aimed his harangue at Jefferson and his Secretary of State, James Madison, to whom Randolph referred collectively as the "Executive" who "will lord it over you."[14] In short, Randolph accused Jefferson of violating separation of powers principles just as Jefferson had accused Hamilton. If one assumes Randolph to have been correct, Jefferson's divergence from his earlier principles may be seen as yet another example of power's ability to corrupt. However, Randolph's accusation was too simple, because the forces that influenced Jefferson were subtle and complex. Barren assertions about the separation of power, its players, and the forces that influenced them fail to capture the complexity of the debate.

The Federal City as a Symbol of
the Separation of Powers

The Jefferson administration was the first to start out in the
new "federal city," designed by French-born engineer Major Pierre C. L'Enfant. Though never fully realized, L'Enfant's plan physically separated the powers and thus,
intentionally or not, gave a geographic expression to a political concept. The Congress and the President's House
were about a mile apart—"a separation so great," as one
architectural critic writes, "that the reciprocal relationship
is almost lost."[15] The "Judiciary Court" was probably to
have its own building in between the Capitol and the executive mansion in what almost from the beginning has been
called Judiciary Square.[16] The most prominent point in
L'Enfant's design was Capitol Hill—"a pedestal waiting for
a superstructure."[17] From there a broad avenue (now the
Mall) was to lead to the executive mansion. As James Sterling Young has noted: "Not only distance but formality and
visibility were apparently considered appropriate for the
relations between Congress and the President, access being
provided by a broad avenue suitable for communication of
a ceremonial nature. 'No message to nor from the President
is to be made,' L'Enfant explained, 'without a sort of decorum.' "[18]

It is ironic that a scheme that can be interpreted as
faithfully repeating the organizing principles of the constitutional plan for government[19] in fact replicated baroque
design motifs "originally conceived to magnify the glories
of despotic kings."[20] L'Enfant grew up in Versailles, and his
plan for Washington has remarkable parallels to that of

Versailles: the Capitol building corresponds to the palace, the President's House to the Trianon, and the Mall to the axes of the canals.[21]

In the event, only the locations of the Capitol itself and the executive mansion reflected L'Enfant's original concept. The Supreme Court remained provisionally housed in the Capitol well into the twentieth century, and the Mall took the place of L'Enfant's great ceremonial street. The physical separation of executive and legislature, however, was for many years even more extreme than that envisaged by L'Enfant. Pennsylvania Avenue was no more than a mud road leading through a swamp. "Considering the difficulties of transportation," historian Dumas Malone has commented, "it was a long mile between Capitol Hill and the President's House, around which the chief departmental offices were clustered. There could be no doubt that the legislative and executive branches were separate."[22]

Jefferson's First Annual Message: A Change in Convention

L'Enfant's notion of ceremonial decorum fell victim not only to the mud but also to "Mr." Jefferson's desire to change the manner in which President and Congress interacted. In the period immediately following the formation of the federal government, the question of physical interaction between Congress and the executive branch was seen as surprisingly significant in separation of powers terms. How should messages be handled, what communications should be oral, which should be in writing? As we saw President Washington grapple with the question in Chapter 2, the underlying concern was one of undue influence on the part of the executive. There was also the question of which of the ceremonial trappings of the monarchy were worth adapting to a republican setting. John Adams, as president of the Senate, had fought for "dignified and respectable government." He wanted President Washington to be treated in a regal fashion.[23]

Washington and Adams had addressed the Congress annually in person. In return, its members had waited as a body on the President with a formal response to his address. Jefferson decided not to follow these precedents. Instead, he sent annual messages in writing to which no answer was due. Jefferson's successors would observe this practice for more than a century, until Woodrow Wilson. The following explanation in a letter to Aaron Burr as president of the Senate accompanied Jefferson's first annual message: "SIR: The circumstances under which we find ourselves placed rendering inconvenient the mode heretofore practiced of making by personal address the first communication between the legislative and executive branches, I have adopted that by message, as used on all subsequent occasions through the session. In doing this, I have had principal regard to the convenience of the legislature, to the economy of their time, to their relief from the embarrassment of immediate answers on subjects not yet fully before them, and to the benefits thence resulting to the public affairs."[24]

This seemingly small step raises a number of interesting issues. Jefferson's justification mentions the legislators' convenience (if he does not go, they also do not have to traverse the swamps) and the "embarrassment" that is inherent in a formal response, which itself was a relic from the conventions of the British monarchy. A letter to Benjamin Rush gave a more political explanation: "By sending a message, instead of making a speech at the opening of the session, I have prevented the bloody conflict to which the making [of] an answer would have committed them. They consequently were able to set into real business at once, without losing 10 or 12 days in combating an answer."[25] The implication is that the change in style was a strategy to manage conflict.

Jefferson's reform, certainly in accord with his own sense of republican simplicity, was also responsive to a request made in the spring of 1801 by Nathaniel Macon, of North Carolina, who later that year would be elected Speaker of the new House.[26] A Republican representative from Pennsylvania, Michael Leib, greeted the reform with the following panegyric: "All the pomp and pageantry, which once dishonored our republican institutions are buried in the tomb of the Capulets. Instead of an address to both houses of Congress made by a President, who was drawn to the Capitol by six horses, and followed by the creatures of his nostrils, and gaped at by a wondering multitude, we had a message delivered by his private Secretary, containing every thing necessary for a great and good man to say, and every thing which embraced the benefit and the comfort of the people."[27]

By forgoing the theatrical aspects of presidential addresses, Jefferson also avoided the personal embarrassment of having to perform before an audience in spite of the stage fright that ordinarily seized him.[28] Jefferson was "an anxious orator," guttural and inarticulate, whose First Inaugural was delivered "at such a whisper that most in attendance could not hear a word he said."[29]

Some may view Jefferson's decision as appropriately deferential to the legislature. The Georgia constitution of 1777 had *required* that all communications between the executive and legislative bodies be in writing.[30] However, as Jay Fliegelman has shown, the matter is actually more ambiguous. According to Fliegelman, John Adams could argue that he was the better "republican" though labeled a monarchist by the Jeffersonians:

> Adams asserted that in "point of republicanism" the essential difference between Adams and Jefferson was "the difference between speeches and [written] messages. I was a monarchist because I thought a speech more manly, more respectful to Congress and the nation. Jefferson . . . preferred messages." In implying the ontological superiority of the oral over the written, Adams asserted his priority over Jefferson. For Adams, presidential addresses did not revisit the stagecraft of monarchy, but opened a dialogue with Congress.[31]

In short, the enigmatic aspects of Jefferson once again pose a puzzle. Alexander Hamilton, in his review of the message for the *New York-Evening Post,* left it "to the conjectures of the curious" whether Jefferson's decision to transmit a message instead of delivering a speech "has proceeded from pride or from humility, from a temperate love of reform, or from a wild spirit of innovation."[32]

Jefferson's first annual message to Congress raised two issues directly pertaining to executive-congressional relations: the war power and the spending power. Both of these issues, together with a third—the President's power to make treaties—tested the notion of separation of power during Jefferson's presidency.

The War Power:
The Conflict at Tripoli

The Barbary Powers occupied American foreign policy more or less continuously for about thirty years beginning in 1784. In dealing with piracy in the Mediterranean, the United States followed the example of most European powers: it paid ransom and tribute to the Ottoman regencies of Algiers, Tunis, and Tripoli. By the turn of the century the bey of Tripoli became publicly dissatisfied with the size of his share of the payment and declared war. When this news reached the United States, Jefferson and his cabinet, on May 15, 1801, decided to dispatch the Navy to the Mediterranean. Congress was, of course, not in session: after his inauguration on March 4, Jefferson had no legislature to cope with until December, when the Seventh Congress assembled and what the President satirically referred to as "our winter campaign" began.[33]

In his first annual message that December, Jefferson reported on the engagement of the American schooner *Enter-*

prise with a Tripolitan cruiser. After a brief battle the *Enterprise* captured, disarmed, and released the enemy vessel and all her crew. No lives were lost.[34] Jefferson said:

> Unauthorized by the constitution, without the sanction of Congress, to go out beyond the line of defence, the vessel being disabled from committing further hostilities, was liberated with its crew. The legislature will doubtless consider whether, by authorizing measures of offence, also, they will place our force on an equal footing with that of its adversaries. I communicate all material information on this subject, that in the exercise of the important function considered by the constitution to the legislature exclusively, their judgment may form itself on a knowledge and consideration of every circumstance of weight.[35]

What is surprising is the narrow construction Jefferson gave his power to seize an enemy ship and its crew. He seemed to deny such power in the President because Congress had given "no sanction." This was contrary to the position taken by all members of the cabinet other than Attorney General Levi Lincoln in the meeting of May 15.[36] The orders issued by Acting Secretary of the Navy Samuel Smith to Commodore Richard Dale provided for sinking, burning, or destroying ships and vessels in case "of their declaring War or committing hostilities."[37] As it turned out, the bey of Tripoli had declared war on May 14. After Jefferson learned about Tripoli's declaration of war, he wrote Madison in September: "What a pity [Commodore Dale] did not know of the [declaration of] war, that he might have taken their admiral and his ship."[38] This comment suggests a legal position different from the one advanced in the message.

Alexander Hamilton published a lengthy commentary on the passage on Tripoli that appeared in the President's first annual message. Pretending to be "anxious for the safety of our government," Hamilton remarked that "we are presented with one of the most singular paradoxes, ever advanced by a man claiming the character of a statesman. When analyzed, it amounts to nothing less than this, that *between* two nations there may exist a state of complete war on the one side—of peace on the other."[39]

Among the cabinet members, Albert Gallatin was most forceful in expressing his belief that it was not necessary to obtain a legislative sanction to use force: "whenever war does exist, whether by the declaration of the United States or by the declaration or act of a foreign nation, I think that the Executive has a right, and is in duty bound, to apply the public force which he may have the means legally to employ, in the most effective manner to annoy the enemy."[40] Gallatin formulated his position in comments on the draft of Jefferson's second annual message and convinced the President to omit language that suggested the need for congressional authority to act offensively in case of war declared or waged by other Barbary powers.[41] He wrote Jefferson: "It is true that the message of last year adopted a different construction of the Constitution; but how that took place I do not recollect. The instructions given to the commanders to release the crews of captured vessels were merely because we did not know what to do with them."[42]

Abraham Sofaer has speculated that Jefferson took the position that he lacked the power to act offensively against a nation that had both declared and made war on the United States, because he wanted Congress' explicit approval of military action in order to share responsibility with Congress.[43] Given that Congress eventually did grant the President authority "to cause to be done all such . . . acts of precaution or hostility as the state of war will justify, and may, in his opinion, require,"[44] this interpretation is plausible enough. The matter, however, is somewhat more complicated.

Jefferson came to the Tripoli issue with considerable prior experience from his days as Secretary of State. His willingness to take steps for the protection of American commerce in the Mediterranean by sending the Navy even though he lacked express legislative authority[45] indicates clearly that he did not shy away from taking action. On the other hand, his overall deference to Congress is quite consistent, as we saw in an earlier chapter, with positions he and President Washington took in relation to the Barbary Powers while Jefferson was Secretary of State. The administration's general inclination was to defer to congressional judgment and to provide Congress with the necessary information for arriving at that judgment. In 1790 Jefferson, in a report on Mediterranean trade, had told the Congress: "Upon the whole, it rests with Congress to decide between war, tribute, and ransom, as the means of re-establishing our Mediterranean commerce. If war, they will consider how far our own resources shall be called forth."[46] Jefferson, while not hesitating to take a stand and, where necessary, action, nevertheless preferred a mandate from those charged, in terms of his inaugural address, "with the sovereign functions of legislation." Since Congress would end up having to pay for military action, the extent to which resources were to be committed was for Congress to decide, not just as a matter of prudence but as a matter of the constitutional allocation of powers "[u]pon the whole." In 1792 Jefferson had gone so far as to advise President Washington to consult not only the Senate but also the House over treaty negotiations with Algiers because the Representatives would have to appropriate money for ransom and tribute.

When he himself became President, Jefferson continued to act with considerable circumspection on matters of war and peace. For instance, his pursuit of the eventually successful war with Tripoli was authorized by legislation of February 6, 1802. Even Abraham Sofaer, who believes that Jefferson abandoned "Republican ideology" toward the end of his presidency, concedes that "Jefferson had prior congressional approval for virtually all the broad objectives he sought."[47] The fact of the matter is that the "embarrassment" Jefferson suffered on account of being charged with inconsistency[48] resulted at least partially from the exacting standards he had pronounced. The controversy over appropriations specificity provides a prime illustration.

The Spending Power:
Specificity and Deficiency of Appropriations

The subject of congressional control over resource appropriations was the second major separation of powers issue addressed in Jefferson's first annual message. Jefferson put forward proposals that were truly extraordinary coming from the head of the executive branch:

> In our care . . . of the public contributions intrusted to our direction, it would be prudent to multiply barriers against their dissipation, by appropriating specific sums to every specific purpose susceptible of definition; by disallowing applications of money varying from the appropriation in object, or transcending it in amount; by reducing the undefined field of contingencies, and thereby circumscribing discretionary powers over money; and by bringing back to a single department all accountabilities for money where the examination may be prompt, efficacious, and uniform.[49]

In short, Jefferson recommended that the power of the executive branch to exercise discretion in the spending of money be curtailed and that the legislature make definite decisions about resource allocation by increasing appropriations specificity.

What the President had to say on the subject of appropriations came at the urging of Albert Gallatin, who, as the fierce Republican opposition leader, had sought to implement the rule of law in government spending.[50] Jefferson routinely invited the members of his cabinet to make comments on the drafts of his annual messages,[51] and Gallatin commented on the President's draft of the first annual message, which made no reference to the subject of appropriations specificity. Gallatin told the President: "There is but one subject not mentioned in the message which I feel extremely anxious to see recommended. It is, generally, that Congress should adopt such measures as will effectually guard against misapplication of public moneys . . . The great characteristic, the flagrant vice, of the late Administration has been total disregard of laws, and application of public moneys by the Departments to objects for which they were not appropriated."[52] Jefferson's message tracks the details of what Gallatin went on to propose.

Hamilton saw the President's recommendations on appropriations specificity as a "deliberate design in the present Chief Magistrate to arraign the former administrations." He characterized the conceptions put forward as "crude and chimerical" and, invoking his own expertise in the area of government finance, took the stance of the elder and wiser statesman in predicting that the experiment would be found "impracticable and injurious; especially in seasons and in situations, when the public service demands activity and exertion."[53]

Gallatin, on the other hand, believed he could combine the rule of law in government expenditures with practicality. He acknowledged that in the past, under the construction given the Army and Navy appropriations acts by the Treasury, "it seems to have been generally understood, that the whole of the monies . . . were to be considered as making but one general appropriation for each of those two objects." In an 1802 response to a House Committee on Investigation, he declared the "most apparent defects in the present arrangements" to be "a want of specification in the several appropriations, defined by law with such precision, as not to leave it in the power of the secretary of the treasury, to affix an arbitrary construction, and to blend together objects which might be kept distinct, without any inconvenience." Gallatin was also concerned about the relative lack of accountability on the part of the War and Navy secretaries for moneys drawn from the Treasury.[54]

Among the remedies he proposed was "that it be enacted, by a general law, that every distinct sum, appropriated by any law, for an object distinctly specified in the law, shall be applicable only to that object." However, far from being "impractical," Gallatin went on to say: "as laws can be executed only so far as they are practicable, and unavoidable deviations will promote a general relaxation, it will be expedient, in the several appropriations laws, especially for the navy and war Departments, not to subdivide the appropriations, beyond what is substantially useful and necessary."[55]

As it turned out, the issue was difficult, if not intractable, even for an administration that was bent on a fairly strict construction of the constitutional allocation of power over money. As early as April 1802, a bill was reported that meant to assure control over expenditures. The bill provided that "every distinct sum of money, which during the present session of congress has been, *or which by any law may hereafter be appropriated for an object distinctly specified, shall be applicable only to such object.*"[56]

Although Congress did not enact the bill, it did in 1802 change the appropriations formulas in the appropriation acts and thus renewed the reforms that Gallatin had first pursued in 1797. Whereas previous language seemed to be appropriating lump sums for the Army and for the Navy, the new enacting clauses forwent the mention of an aggregate sum and used the formula "the following *sums* be, and the same hereby are *respectively* appropriated, that is to say."[57] The change lies in the use of the plural "sums" instead of the singular "sum" and in the addition of the modifier "respectively."

Thus, while, for instance, the Military Appropriations Act of 1801 read "the *sum* of two millions, ninety-three thousand and one dollars, be and *is hereby appropriated;* that is to say," the 1802 legislation employed the language, "That for defraying the several expenses of the military establishment . . . the following *sums* be, and the same are *respectively* appropriated, that is to say."[58] There were a few vagaries in the process, but by 1804 all general appropriations acts essentially used the same approach. Itemization on the military side of the government remained much less specific than on the civil side. Gallatin preferred this bow to expediency and to his colleagues in the cabinet over a de facto relaxation that might have followed from being too strict and from attempting the impossible. In his view, a generally accepted disregard of appropriation laws in the prior administrations had placed the executive branch above the law.

The issue of specificity arose also with regard to the size of contingency appropriations. Here Gallatin fought very hard against lump-sum payments, especially with Navy Secretary Samuel Smith. In an 1803 letter to Jefferson, in which he strenuously objected to Navy requests for contingencies, Gallatin expressed the need to be consistent with positions expressed while in opposition: "I hope that you will pardon my stating my opinion on that subject, when you recollect with what zeal and perseverance I opposed for a number of years, whilst in Congress, similar loose demands for money."[59] Gallatin engaged in "confidential intercourse" on these matters with Republican members of Congress, especially in "free communications of facts and opinions" to John Randolph, of Ways and Means.[60] Leonard White credited the intimate and continuous relations between the Secretary of the Treasury and both houses of Congress with facilitating "the extraordinary compliance that Jefferson drew from his party followers in the two Houses."[61]

Although "the process was less one of confrontation than of cooperation,"[62] especially in the early years of the administration, the question of appropriations specificity remained a core separation of powers issue throughout the years of the Jefferson administration, particularly in connection with naval appropriations. The irony of the matter was that the Federalists continued to adhere to Hamiltonian notions of flexibility and enjoyed every apparent Republican lapse from rigorous adherence to the doctrine of congressional control. For instance, in April 1806 David Williams, a newly elected Republican member of Congress from South Carolina, wanted to divide into specifics a lump-sum item of more than $400,000 for "repair of vessels, store rent, pay of armorers, freight, and other contingent expenses" because he opposed "the system."[63] Congressman Samuel Dana, a leading Federalist from Connecticut, said that the proposed amendment was "warranted by the former usage of the House" and by Jefferson's first annual message. "[H]e considered the gentleman from South Carolina as bringing up this question directly before the House: Will you adhere to specific appropriations, or will you abandon them?" Dana went on to say that he did not favor specific appropriations in relation to the Navy or the Army.[64] Williams' motion lost, fifty-one to thirty-two.[65]

A corollary to specificity was deficiency: what should happen when specific appropriations were insufficient to cover necessary expenditures? When Congressman Jacob Crowinshield, a Republican from Massachusetts, that same April of 1806, moved that the so-called Mediterranean Fund be continued for three years, John Randolph rose in fierce and successful opposition, expressing his disenchantment with the progress that had been made since 1801. Randolph had started out as Republican leader in the House and as chairman of Ways and Means. In these roles he had administered the doctrine of congressional control with a measure of flexibility. After he broke with the administration over the Yazoo affair and other matters, he became its leading critic on issues of adherence to appropriations. In his response to Crowinshield's motion, Randolph expressed his hope that the amendment would not be agreed to, as that would lessen the control of the House over expenditures: they would not be able to revoke the grant without the Senate's concurrence. He then continued: "It is true that we have some check in making appropriations; but appropriations have become a matter of form, or less than the shadow of a shade, a mere cobweb of defence against expenditures. You have fixed limits, but the expenditure exceeds the appropriations; and those who disburse the money, are like a saucy boy who knows that his grandfather will gratify him, and over-runs the sum allowed him at pleasure. As to appropriations I have no faith in them."[66]

These matters were considered to involve the constitutional structure rather than mere politics. This view gains strong support from the fact that in the very last days of the Jefferson administration Congress finally enacted the framework legislation on appropriations that Gallatin had sought back in 1802. In both the Senate and the House, new allegations had been made about illegal military disbursements.[67] Gallatin had begun to demand as early as 1802 (after the changes in the enacting clauses of the appropriations acts) that warrants from the War and Navy departments detail the specific appropriations against which they were drawn.[68] He now proposed to George Campbell, the chairman of Ways and Means, that the law should require that "all contracts drawn by the Secretaries of War and of the Navy . . . should specify the particular appropriation to which the same should be charged." He made additional suggestions for tightening accountability overall and also referred Campbell to the more general recommendations he had made in March 1802.[69]

While otherwise preoccupied with repeal of Jefferson's greatest foreign policy failure, the Embargo Act,[70] Congress found time to do more or less exactly what Gallatin had requested and, furthermore, finally enacted the framework provision that implemented what Gallatin had wanted in the first year following the "revolution of 1800." The "regulations to guard the expenditures of the public money"[71] came in "An Act further to amend the several acts for the establishment and regulation of the Treasury, War and Navy departments." The 1809 statute passed in the evening hours of the last day of the session and provided that "the sums appropriated by law for each branch of expenditure in the several departments shall be *solely* applied to the objects for which they are respectively appropriated." The legislation also conferred limited authority on the President to shift funds within departments "if in his opinion necessary," but only when Congress was in recess.[72]

This latter provision is of particular interest since it made an effort to subject even emergencies, such as the *Chesapeake* confrontation, to the rule of law by granting the executive explicit legislative authority to deviate from the specificity of appropriations. Notwithstanding that the Jeffersonians had been through eight years of "seasons and . . . situations" that demanded "activity and exertion," they continued to believe that "[t]he exigencies of the public service" could be attained within the framework of general rules.[73]

This emphasis on rules, present even at the end of Jefferson's presidency, had been the target of Hamilton's criticism from the beginning. In his comprehensive and detailed examination of Jefferson's first annual message, Hamilton had written eloquently concerning the subject of appropriations specificity:

It is certainly possible to do too much as well as too little; to embarrass, if not defeat the good which may be done, by attempting more than is practicable; or to overbalance that good by evils accruing from an excess of regulation. Men of business know this to be the case in the ordinary affairs of life: how much more must it be so, in the extensive and complicated concerns of an Empire? To reach and not to pass the salutary medium is the province of sound judgment: To miss the point will ever be the lot of those who, enveloped all their lives in the mists of theory, are constantly seeking for an ideal perfection which never was and never will be attainable in reality. It is about this medium, not about general principles, that those in power in our government have differed.[74]

Hamilton did not understand that the dispute between him and Gallatin was not over "ideal perfection" against "sound judgment," but over the extent to which sound judgment depended on adherence to general principles. Neither Gallatin nor Jefferson himself got lost "in the mists of theory" when it came to governing. Indeed, as to the "extensive and complicated concerns of an Empire," Jefferson demonstrated his capacity to be at Hamilton's "salutary medium" in the manner in which he handled the Louisiana Purchase.[75]

The Louisiana Purchase

With respect to the Louisiana Purchase, attention has for the most part focused on the constitutional power to acquire territory and on Jefferson's change of mind as to the need for a constitutional amendment.[76] Indeed, Jefferson's reputation as President has been closely tied to the fact that he overcame his constitutional scruples when he followed the lead of Madison, who had no qualms about expansion and the means of achieving it.[77] Concerning the separation of powers, on the other hand, the tangle of principle, serendipity, and sheer contingency, which the purchase represented, mostly tested precedent rather than constitutional convictions. Controversies in the prior administrations, such as that over the Jay Treaty, had helped to, if not solve, at least clarify issues.

In his second annual message, delivered in December 1802, Jefferson reserved one short paragraph to the subject of Louisiana: "The cession of the Spanish province of Louisiana to France, which took place in the course of the late war, will, if carried into effect, make a change in the aspect of our foreign relations which will doubtless have just weight in any deliberations of the legislature connected with that subject."[78] The legislature did indeed deliberate immediately, especially on the matter that Jefferson had failed to mention: the suspension of the right of deposit in New Orleans by the Spanish intendant two months earlier. The House asked for papers on Spain's action and furthermore engaged in lengthy debate whether it had the power to ask for diplomatic exchanges and whether it was expedient to do so.[79]

The House also passed a partially sycophantic "sense of the House" resolution in support of the right of navigation and commerce on the Mississippi. The resolution included language to the effect that the House was "relying, with perfect confidence, on the vigilance and wisdom of the Executive." A motion to strike these words lost, fifty-three to thirty,[80] enabling Representative Richard Henry Dana to exclaim a few days later, "What! 'relying with perfect confidence in the Executive'—is this the language of the Constitution, as it respects any man?"[81]

Finally, Congress appropriated $2 million for the vaguely stated purpose of defraying "expenses which may be incurred in relation to the intercourse between the United States and foreign nations . . . to be applied under the direction of the President of the United States." The appropriation was to enable the President to negotiate with France and Spain for the purchase of New Orleans and the Floridas. Interestingly, Jefferson sought and obtained the blessing of the House, although strictly speaking it was only for the Senate to "advise" on treaties. The House committee which had been concerned with the matter allowed that they had "no information before them, to ascertain the amount for which the purchase can be made, but it is hoped that with the assistance of two millions of dollars in hand, this will not be unreasonable."[82] Both houses made the appropriation in secret sessions.[83] Jefferson supposedly told Senator William Plumer, a Federalist from New Hampshire, that "[a] great point [has now been] gained; a new precedent established in our government—the passage of an important law by Congress, in *secret session*."[84] Governmental practice, as early as the First Congress of the United States, had included secret expenditures for vaguely stated purposes as well as secret communications. It was assumed, as indicated by the journal secrecy clause in Article I, Section 5 of the Constitution, that in some circumstances the American people had a need for secrecy as compelling as their need for information.[85]

Concerning the matter of information more generally, it is important to remind ourselves that the conditions under which communications took place often hampered checks and balances. In separation of powers terms, if the legislature was presented with a *fait accompli,* so, in almost all essential respects, was the head of the executive branch.

There are a few highlights to note from the course of the Louisiana Purchase negotiations.[86] James Monroe, the special envoy sent to join Minister to France Robert Livingstone for the purpose of negotiating with the French government, arrived in Paris on April 12, 1803, one day after Talleyrand had asked Livingstone whether the United States would buy all of Louisiana. Irving Brant has argued that the French inquiry was in response to an April 7 London *Times* account of the saber rattling actions of the U.S. Senate.[87] Apparently, through this newspaper Napoleon had learned that on February 25 the Senate had unanimously called on the President "to take effectual measures" to arm 80,000 militia as well as to make other preparations for war with France.[88] On April 30, 1803, the parties signed a treaty in Paris for the American purchase of Louisiana. The final purchase price was $15 million. On June 25 Secretary of State Madison, by now aware of the French interest in selling the whole of Louisiana but unaware that a treaty had already been signed, wrote Monroe: "The dawn of your negotiations has given much pleasure and much expectation . . . The purchase of the country beyond the Mississippi was not contemplated in your powers because it was not deemed at this time within the frame of probability . . . It is presumed that the defect will not be permitted either by yourself or by the French government to embarrass, much less suspend, your negotiations on the enlarged scale."[89]

Jefferson learned of the treaty on July 3, and the *National Intelligencer* published the news on Independence Day.[90] The official papers arrived on July 14. Since the treaty required the exchange of ratifications within six months of its April 30 date, the President convened Congress three weeks early, on October 17.[91] In his third annual message, the President reminded Congress that it had given "sanction" to the acquisition of New Orleans "and of other possessions in that quarter" through the "provisional appropriation of two millions of dollars." Observing a strict procedural sequence, Jefferson wrote that once the treaty instruments "have received the constitutional sanction of the senate, they will without delay be communicated to the representatives also, for the exercise of their functions, as to those conditions which are within the powers vested by the constitution in Congress."[92]

The Senate gave its consent on October 20, and the next day the exchange of ratifications created a binding treaty obligation for the United States before congressional action. On October 22 Jefferson sent the conventions to the House "for consideration in your Legislative capacity,"[93] though without the diplomatic documents that he had provided the Senate. On October 25 a sideshow took place that raised issues of consistency and precedent. Roger Griswold, a Federalist congressman from Connecticut, moved that the President be requested to provide treaty documents that would establish whether the United States had effectively acquired title from France in relation to Spain.[94]

Seven years earlier, in March 1796, President Washington had refused to provide the House of Representatives of
the Fourth Congress with the Jay Treaty papers, invoking
the constitutional separation of powers that gave the House
no role in the treaty-making process. At that time the Republicans had favored the resolution calling for the papers.[95] Now the leader of the Republicans in the House,
John Randolph, who had not been a member of the Fourth
Congress, objected on the ground that delay would jeop-
ardize the best interest of the union. He lamely distinguished the Jay Treaty precedent by arguing that that had
been an unpopular treaty, whereas this one was "hailed by
the acclamations of the nation."[96]

John Smilie, a Republican from Pennsylvania, reminded
Roger Griswold that he, Griswold, had been on the other
side of the issue in the Jay Treaty case. Smilie himself had
served in the Third Congress but not in the Fourth. Smilie
asked rhetorically what President Washington's opinion
had been and went on: "Not that I approve of it, or am
governed by it; though it ought, in my opinion, to be a rule
on this occasion to those who coincided with him."[97] He
then proceeded to read the full text of Washington's message rejecting the request for the Jay Treaty papers.

This appeal to consistency could, of course, apply with
equal force to the Republicans, and, indeed, must have,
since the Griswold motion lost by the narrow margin of two
votes, 59 to 57,[98] even though there were 103 Republicans in
the House, versus only 39 Federalists.[99] As Dumas Malone
has pointed out, the defeat of the Griswold resolution
spared Jefferson the embarrassment of saying that he either

could not or would not produce the documents.[100] After all, as Secretary of State he had come out in favor of interpreting the role of the House of Representatives in foreign affairs liberally. Actually, even in the case of Louisiana it appears, from comments made by both Madison and Gallatin on the first draft of the President's third annual message, that Jefferson originally intended to lay the treaty before both houses simultaneously in order to avoid delay. Both Madison and Gallatin, however, objected on constitutional grounds. Gallatin wrote: "The House of Representatives neither can nor ought to act on the treaty until after it is a treaty."[101] Madison stated even more directly: "the theory of our constitution does not seem to have provided for the influence of deliberations . . . of the House of Representatives on a Treaty depending in the Senate."[102]

On October 27 the House took up a Senate bill "to enable the President of the United States to take possession of and occupy the territories ceded by France to the United States." The bill included a section that subjected all military, civil, and judicial powers in the new territories to the direction of the President "until Congress shall have made provision for the temporary government of the said Territories."[103] The first to speak was John Randolph, who, though the Republican leader, objected, on separation of powers grounds, to the delegation as too sweeping. He stressed that if the bill was adopted, the executive branch with a small minority of either house could prevent the repeal of the delegation. He therefore moved an amendment that terminated the delegation at "the expiration of the present session of Congress," unless Congress made an earlier "provision for temporary government."[104] Roger Griswold found the compromise insufficient: "we are about making the President the legislator, the judge, and the executive of this territory. I do not . . . understand that, according to the Constitution, we have a right to make him legislator, judge, and executive, in any territory belonging to the United States."[105]

It is of great interest that Congress debated Griswold's objection at some length. Although it was not a partisan issue, some Federalists had their fun at Republicans' expense. Federalist Representative Manasseh Cutler thought the President had been "made as despotic as the Grand Turk,"[106] and Senator Plumer observed wryly: "Had such a bill been passed by federalists, the Democrats would have denounced it as *monarchal;* but when enacted by the *exclusive friends of* the people, it is pure *republicanism.*"[107] In the end, the Senate bill was amended as suggested by John Randolph after further language had been added that made it clear that the purpose of the delegation was to maintain and protect "the inhabitants of Louisiana in the full enjoyment of their liberty, property, and religion."[108]

Before the matter was voted on, a freshman Republican from Virginia, John Jackson, summed up what, from the vantage point of congressional separation of powers practices, were concerns even for members of the majority:

> When I recur to the Constitution, I find that though it does not expressly say, the Legislative, Executive, and Judicial powers shall be distinct, as some constitutions lately formed do, yet it amounts in fact to the

same thing, by delegating special powers exclusively to particular departments. I believe also the President to be inimical to the extension of Executive power. I am not afraid of delegating such power, if not inconsistent with the Constitution, because I have so much confidence in the President, as to be convinced that he would not abuse it. But I believe principle ought, under all circumstances, to be respected; and under present circumstances, though we may have a President so congenial to our wishes. What, if hereafter we should deem it important to oppose the delegation of such power? gentlemen, in favor of such delegation will say, here is a precedent set by yourselves, and thus preclude us, on the score of consistency, from opposing the measure.[109]

As Representative Jackson worried about principle, precedent, and consistency in separation of powers practice, so, that fall, did his President worry about constitutional construction. Preferring a constitutional amendment in order to legitimate the acquisition of Louisiana, Jefferson wrote to Wilson Cary Nicholas: "I had rather ask an enlargement of power from the nation, where it is found necessary, than to assume it by construction which would make our powers boundless. Our peculiar security is in possession of a written Constitution. Let us not make it a blank paper by construction."[110]

Earlier that summer the President had been struck by the "scrape" in which he found himself with respect to Louisiana. If all authority was delegated, by the medium of the

Constitution, from the people, what were the responsibilities of the country's "servants"? In a remarkable letter to John Breckenridge, dated Monticello, August 12, 1803, Jefferson wrote: "The Executive in seizing the fugitive occurrence which so much advances the good of their country, have done an act beyond the Constitution. The Legislature in casting behind them metaphysical subtleties, and risking themselves like faithful servants, must ratify & pay for it, and throw themselves on their country for doing for them unauthorized what we know they would have done for themselves had they been in a situation to do it."[111] After Jefferson had left public service he put it more bluntly than most: "To lose our country by a scrupulous adherence to written law, would be to lose the law itself, with life, liberty, property and all those who are enjoying them with us; thus absurdly sacrificing the end to the means."[112]

Was fortuity turning Jefferson into a "monarch" after all? Hardly, although he persistently tended to exaggerate the differences between "the monarchist" Hamilton and himself. There can be little question that, on the whole, Jefferson strove to abide by the letter and spirit of the Constitution. While he was the most forceful chief executive yet, he worried more than Hamilton about his accountability to the people whose agent he was. It was that agency relationship rather than Hamiltonian confidence in Hamiltonian "sound judgment" that offered Jefferson the hope of "indemnity," of ultimate vindication for legal trespasses. For the interpretation of that agency relationship, the written "instructions"—that is, the Constitution—remained of prime importance to Jefferson throughout his life. How-

ever, Jefferson saw his role as "the case of a guardian, invest-
ing the money of his ward in purchasing an important
adjacent territory; & saying to him when of age, I did this
for your good; I pretend to no right to bind you: you may
disavow me, and I must get out of the scrape as I can: I
thought it my duty to risk myself for you."[113]

The analogy of the guardian was rather maladroit. After
all, the President, the Congress, and the judiciary are not
the guardians of a minor, but the agents of the sovereign.
The 1780 constitution of Massachusetts had formulated the
principle: "All power residing originally in the people, and
being derived from them, the several magistrates and
officers of government, vested with authority, whether legislative, executive, or judicial, are their substitutes and
agents, and are at all times accountable to them."[114] But
then Jefferson's reference to guardianship was perhaps no
more than a metaphorical expression of his lifelong am-
bivalence about the pursuits and burdens of public life that
"had nothing in them agreeable," as he had said to Washington back in 1792.[115]

To Jefferson, being President felt like being "in a scrape."
He used an even more dramatic simile when, in 1809, he did
get out of the scrape for good, believing, or maybe only
hoping, that on the whole the people had approved of his
agency. During his last days in office he wrote P. S. DuPont
de Nemours: "Never did a prisoner, released from his
chains, feel such relief as I shall on shaking off the shackles
of power . . . I thank God for the opportunity of retiring
from [political passions] without censure, and carrying
with me the most consoling proofs of public approba-

tion."[116] The "shackles of power" Jefferson shook off were not the chains imposed by constitutional constraints, such as those incident to the separation of powers, but to his mind it was power itself that had chained him. "Mr." Jefferson did indeed, as a President should, think of himself as an agent rather than as a principal.

$$\frac{5}{\widehat{\text{个}}}$$

THE JUDICIARY ACT OF 1789
AND JUDICIAL INDEPENDENCE

Among the more peculiar aspects of American historical consciousness is the fact that we celebrated the bicentennial of the Bill of Rights in 1991 rather than, by analogy with the bicentennial of the Constitution, in 1989. Congressional agreement on the constitutional amendments was reached on September 24, 1789, and, but for the nonratification of two amendments, the Bill of Rights stands as adopted in 1789—at least as far as its text is concerned. If we viewed 1789 as the year in which both the Judiciary Act and the Bill of Rights originated, we might give more weight to those elements of the Judiciary Act that are closely related to the Bill of Rights and that tell us much about attitudes toward the judiciary two years after the Constitutional Convention.

On September 21, 1789, the House agreed to the Senate's final version of the Judiciary Act, and on September 24 the Senate agreed to the proposed articles of amendment to the Constitution. Let us recall that of the eight amendments that deal with specifics—that is, not counting the Ninth and Tenth Amendments—five regard matters mostly concerning the courts.

During the summer of 1789, Congress provided for the decision-making procedures of the branches of government by spelling out its interpretation of the constitutional framework. The houses of Congress secured the structure of their own decision-making by developing rules for themselves. As mentioned in Chapter 2, they also regulated executive branch decision-making by enacting the statutes that established the departments of State, War, and the Treasury, their responsibilities, and their procedures. Finally, Congress passed the Judiciary Act, whose proper name is "An Act to establish the Judicial Courts of the United States,"[1] and submitted its constitutional amendments for ratification by the states.[2]

As we saw in Chapter 1, among the amendments proposed by the House of Representatives but not concurred in by the Senate was one that attempted to spell out the framework implied by Articles I, II, and III of the Constitution. James Madison proposed the amendment in response to complaints in some of the ratifying conventions that the Constitution paid insufficient heed to the separation of powers. The amendment's genius was that it seemed to add something merely by saying what went without saying—that the powers delegated by the Constitution were to be exercised "as therein appropriated."[3]

The House agreed to this and the other proposed amendments on August 24 and sent them on to the Senate. The same day, the House began its debate of the judiciary bill. Two days later, in Versailles, the French National Assembly adopted the Declaration of the Rights of Man and of the Citizen, Article 16 of which said: "A society in which the guarantee of rights is not assured, nor the separation of powers provided for, has no constitution."[4]

The question this historical backdrop poses, in separation of powers terms, is simply how the Judiciary Act relates to the notion of an independent judiciary within the context of the last quarter of the eighteenth century. It is my view that the Judiciary Act reflects a more complex concept of the judicial role than Article III of the Constitution. Though consonant with Article III, the Judiciary Act takes into account fears about the judiciary that found little expression in Philadelphia but that also underlie portions of the Bill of Rights.

The Judiciary in France, England, and the United States

For purposes of contrast, comparative observations about constitutional developments in France and in the American states serve as an instructive starting point for this analysis. Probably the most consequential action of the French National Assembly in the summer of 1789 was the decree of August 4–11, which abolished the remnants of feudalism and the venality of judicial offices.[5] The most important of the French courts, the *parlements,* had been composed of councilors whose offices for centuries and up to the French Revolution had been regarded as private property and as inheritable. The *parlements,* which also had rule-making and administrative functions, had been bastions of the *ancien régime,* though not infrequently in conflict with the kings and the policies of their ministries.[6]

When the French revolutionaries reconsidered the relationship between courts and government in light of the doctrine of popular sovereignty and French views of the separation of powers, their version of a judiciary act, the decree of August 16–24, 1790, ordered the judiciary to check neither legislature nor administration.[7] It prohibited the elected judges from directly or indirectly interfering with the legislative power. It prohibited judicial review not only of legislation but also of administrative action. I quote the famous Article 13 of Title II: "Judicial functions are distinct and will always remain separate from administrative functions. Judges may not, under pain of forfeiture of their offices, concern themselves in any manner whatsoever with the operation of the administration, nor shall they summon administrators to appear before them on account of their official functions."[8]

If the French implementation of separation of powers principles reflected considerable concern about a judiciary's potential for thwarting the "general will" as expressed in legislation and administration, the American situation was both simpler and more complicated. It was simpler because English constitutional developments before 1776 had inculcated a preference for an independent judiciary. It was more complicated because it was less than obvious how that preference could be reconciled with the notion that all officers of government, legislative, executive, or judicial, had to be at all times accountable to the source of all power—the people.[9] While the French faced the same issue, the history of their *parlements* had not left them with a deep imprint in favor of judicial independence.

The Glorious Revolution of 1688 and the Act of Settlement of 1701 had established in England what had been fought over even earlier: that judges should serve during "good behavior" *(quam diu se bene gesserint)*.[10] The dispute between the colonies and London was in part over the Crown's unwillingness to recognize the applicability of this principle in the colonies. As the Declaration of Independence shows, George III was accused of having made the judges dependent on his will alone, for the tenure of their offices and for the amount and payment of their salaries.[11] In light of this criticism, it is hardly surprising that the constitutions of eight of the thirteen original states provided for judicial tenure during good behavior.[12] However, there is less here than meets the eye. Just as the Act of Settlement had provided for removal of judges upon the address of both Houses of Parliament, the constitutions of five states possessed a sword of this kind.[13] If we add to this enumeration those states where judges were appointed or elected for a term of years,[14] ten states retained some measure of political control over sitting judges in addition to impeachment. Indeed, of the thirteen original states, only three maintained what might be called an unqualified good-behavior standard. In two of these, Virginia and North Carolina, the legislature chose the judges,[15] while the third, New York, provided for compulsory retirement of judges at age sixty.[16]

The Challenge of an Independent Judiciary

The founding generation was ambivalent about the independence of the judiciary. On the one hand, they thought it the right of every citizen "to be tried by judges as free, impartial, and independent as the lot of humanity will admit," as it was put in the Massachusetts Declaration of Rights.[17] On the other hand, the puzzle was how much separation of powers "the nature of a free government will admit," which was the limiting formula of the New Hampshire Bill of Rights.[18] The dilemma was part and parcel of the larger conundrums: How can one have both stability and change at once? How can one reconcile majority rule with a bill of rights? What does it mean to have separation of powers when there is but one single source of power—the people? If in republican government it is a necessity that the judges follow the letter of the law,[19] it is also a necessity that there be an impartial interpretation of the law.[20] Indeed, the very concept of a written constitution, sharply differentiated from ordinary legislation and consented to by the people or their representatives, made it unavoidable to contemplate the power of judges to set aside laws.[21]

The manner in which Article III of the Constitution viewed the third branch differed considerably from that of the state constitutions from 1776 through 1787. Two aspects of Article III and the discussion of the judiciary in the Constitutional Convention are especially noteworthy in this respect. First, by comparison with all the state constitutions, Article III represents the extreme solution: an appointed judiciary serving at a guaranteed salary for life, subject only to impeachment. Not a single state constitution had gone that far.

Second, when one reviews the debates in the Constitutional Convention, the strength of the commitment to an independent judiciary is striking. Nobody questioned tenure during good behavior. When, at the end of August 1787, John Dickinson of Delaware moved for adoption of the Act of Settlement mechanism for removal of judges upon the address of both houses, Gouverneur Morris declared it to be a contradiction in terms that judges should hold their office during good behavior and yet be removable without a trial. After a short discussion, only Connecticut, arguably the state with the most dependent judiciary, voted in favor of the motion.[22]

About the only explicit discussion of tenure during good behavior came in mid-July, when Madison explained why judges had not been subjected to reappointment at the pleasure of the legislature (the appointment of judges was at this time lodged in the Senate). Judges might be tempted, Madison suggested, to cultivate the legislature by an undue complaisance "and thus render the Legislature the virtual expositor, as well as the maker of the laws."[23] Madison and James Wilson's pet project of including the judiciary in a council of revision was defeated by those who thought it violated the ideal of an independent judiciary.[24] If Madison did not want the *legislators* to become *interpreters* of the law, the opponents of the Council of Revision did not like the idea that *judges* would be involved in the *making* of the laws.

The Constitution's commitment to an independent judiciary is strong and remarkable. We should nevertheless not lose sight of the fact that the independent judiciary envisaged by Article III was seen as an arm of the federal government for the execution of federal policies. While independent in separation-of-powers terms, it was not necessarily thought of as a completely neutral arbiter of legal and constitutional conflicts. Quite the contrary: to many, the independent federal judiciary was the answer to worries about the dependence of state courts.[25] This was nowhere made clearer than in the consideration of the judiciary bill, as the First Congress could no longer avoid the issue of lower federal courts and their jurisdiction.

At the very beginning of the Constitutional Convention, we encounter the first of many debates extending from Philadelphia to the state conventions to the First Congress about whether there should be inferior federal tribunals. Madison argued in Philadelphia what he repeated in New York in 1789: "An effective Judiciary establishment commensurate to the legislative authority, was essential. A Government without a proper Executive & Judiciary would be the mere trunk of a body without arms or legs to act or move."[26] In the debates on the judiciary bill, such members of the First Congress as Madison, Fisher Ames, Theodore Sedgwick, Egbert Benson, and William Loughton Smith dwelt at length on the same point. A one-by-one review of state constitutions led Madison to conclude that the state courts could not be trusted with the execution of federal laws; it would not be "safe" to transfer jurisdiction.[27] Fisher Ames considered it strange to have laws interpreted and executed by those "whom we do not appoint, and cannot control."[28]

When the Massachusetts Declaration of Rights had referred to the right to be tried by judges who were as "free, impartial, and independent as the lot of humanity will admit,"
it had implied the inevitability of some bias and dependence.
From a Federalist perspective, however, the state judges were
problematic not only because of their psychological potential for parochialism, but also because the doctrine of popular sovereignty considered even judges to be merely agents of
the sovereign. The Massachusetts Declaration of Rights used
emphatic language in this respect: all power resides in the
people, and the several magistrates, "whether legislative, executive, or judicial, are their substitutes and agents, and are
at all times accountable to them."[29] William Paterson, Theodore Sedgwick, Fisher Ames, and Elbridge Gerry, among
other members of the First Congress, understood perfectly
well that the supremacy clause of Article VI, even in con-
junction with the required oath, could not magically overcome the ingrained doctrine of popular sovereignty.[30]

Of course, even a federal judiciary appointed by the
national government was not necessarily a panacea for all
the ills of parochialism. In one of the more ingenious and,
as subsequent history illustrates, perceptive contributions
to the debates on the Judiciary Act, William Loughton
Smith of South Carolina attempted to calm fears about the
federal judiciary by pointing out that federal judges, too,
would be dependent and that their very independence
could be employed in the service of that dependence:

[T]he district judge will be elected from among the
citizens of the State where he is to exercise his func-

tions, and will feel every inducement to promote the happiness and protect the liberties of his fellow-citizens. He will be more independent than the State judges, holding his commission during good behaviour, and not influenced by the fear of a diminution of his salary. Trial by jury will be secured in all cases wherein it is provided in the State courts. Should the district judge be under any bias, it is reasonable to suppose it would be rather in favor of his fellow-citizens, than in favor of foreigners, or the United States.[31]

Smith's observation neatly showed that the problem of conflicting loyalties was not necessarily solved by a separate system of federal courts.

The very servant-master relationship that made state judges suspect to the Federalists made the independent judiciary envisaged and implied by Article III troublesome to the Anti-Federalists. The provisions for a national judiciary and its jurisdiction were among the most frequently criticized aspects in the ratification debates. "Brutus," the very able New York critic of the Constitution, turned the independence of the federal judiciary from the virtue the framers proclaimed it to be into a vice: "they have made the judges *independent,* in the fullest sense of the word. There is no power above them, to controul any of their decisions. There is no authority that can remove them, and they cannot be controlled by the laws of the legislature. In short, they are independent of the people, of the legislature, and of every power under heaven." "Brutus" rejected the English analogy because not only did English judges not have the power of judicial review, but their errors were subject to correction by the House of Lords, at that time still thought of as a parliamentary institution.[32]

"Brutus" undoubtedly misconceived the meaning of Article III when he attributed to the federal judges "the power of giving an *equitable* construction to the constitution,"[33]— unless, that is, one assumes that "Brutus" was predicting twentieth-century approaches to constitutional interpretation. However, the equity power of the federal courts was one of the irritants unwittingly created by the drafters of Article III, as was the Supreme Court's power of appellate jurisdiction, "both as to law & fact,"[34] and the omission of the civil jury. One must view these three problems—all addressed by the Judiciary Act—together. They brought forth opposition because they were viewed as indicative of an overbearing judiciary far removed from popular control. Edmund Randolph, at the Virginia ratification convention, summed it all up when he complained, "The judiciary is drawn up in terror."[35]

The three elements had in common that they seemed to increase the power of judges at the cost of popular institutions, especially juries. Put differently, the worry was that the new federal judiciary would be too independent: equity could override the common law; the Supreme Court on appeal could review even facts found by a jury; and, in civil cases, judges might sit without juries. The frequency with which these points were raised was such that, also at the Virginia convention, Edmund Pendleton, a supporter of the Constitution, commented about the "law and fact" language: "Though I dread no danger, I wish these words had been buried in oblivion."[36]

A passage from the Pennsylvania "Democratic Federalist" provides the emotive connotations that the critics pursued:

> The word *appeal* . . . in its proper legal signification includes the *fact* as well as the *law,* and precludes every idea of a trial by jury—It is a word *of foreign growth,* and is only known in England and America in those courts which are governed by the civil or ecclesiastical law of the *Romans.* Those courts have always been considered in England as a grievance, and have all been established by the usurpations of the *ecclesiastical* over the *civil* power. It is well known that the courts of chancery in England were formerly entirely in the hands of *ecclesiastics,* who took advantage of the strict forms of the common law, to introduce a foreign mode of jurisprudence under the specious name of *Equity.* Pennsylvania, the freest of all American States has wisely rejected this establishment, and knows not even the name of a court of chancery—And in fact, there can not be any thing more absurd than a distinction between LAW and EQUITY. It might perhaps have suited those barbarous times when the law of England, like almost every other science, was perplexed with quibbles and *Aristotelian* distinctions, but it would be shameful to keep it up in these more enlightened days. At any rate, it seems to me that there is much more *equity* in a trial by jury, than in an appellate jurisdiction from the fact.[37]

Or, as another Pennsylvanian, William Maclay, put it during the Senate's deliberations on the Judiciary Act: "12 honest Jurors are good Chancellors."[38]

Given the importance of Montesquieu for the implementation of separation of powers notions in the last quarter of the eighteenth century, it is more than a little ironic that the Constitution caused so much opposition by applying to professional judges separation of powers notions that Montesquieu, who had misunderstood English institutions, had originally developed with juries, rather than judges, in mind. Montesquieu wanted the judicial power exercised by persons taken from "the body of the people" for a tribunal to last only as long as necessity required: "By this method of judicial power, so terrible to mankind, not being annexed to any particular state or profession, becomes, as it were, invisible. People have not then the judges continually present to their view; they fear the office, but not the magistrate."[39]

In a way, the Anti-Federalists were the true disciples of Montesquieu in their emphasis on juries as crucial for the separation of powers. "Centinel" expressed this point emotionally when he wrote at the beginning of his critique of the Constitution that he was using his pen with the boldness of a freeman because he knew that juries yet were judges.[40] The notion was that the review of facts by the Supreme Court and the failure to guarantee juries in civil cases amounted to the abolition of jury trials.[41] But, the "Maryland Farmer" stressed,

> [t]he trial by jury is—the democratic branch of the judiciary power—more necessary than representatives

in the legislature; for those usurpations which silently undermine the spirit of liberty, under the sanction of law, are more dangerous than direct and open legislative attacks . . . Destroy juries and every thing is prostrated to judges, who may easily disguise law, by suppressing and varying fact:—Whenever therefore the trial by juries has been abolished, the liberties of the people were soon lost—The judiciary power is immediately absorbed, or placed under the direction of the executive, as example teaches in most of the States of Europe.[42]

The framers of the Constitution were hardly inclined to engineer a reception of the "civil law" or to institute executive control of the judiciary. Yet their version of the separation of powers was perceived as providing for a judiciary that was too independent of the vox populi.

The Judiciary Act's Limitations on Judicial Power

The vehement and widespread opposition to the judicial institutions allegedly implied by Article III was replayed in the debates of the First Congress and was reflected in the provisions of the Judiciary Act as well as those of the Bill of Rights, especially the Sixth and Seventh Amendments. Charles Warren therefore called the Judiciary Act a "compromise measure."[43]

Sections 9, 12, and 13 of the Judiciary Act provided for trial of "issues in fact" by jury, except in admiralty, maritime, and equity cases. The Seventh Amendment even constitutionalized the civil jury. For a short while, the Senate version of the judiciary bill had required juries in equity cases.[44] Section 29, in capital cases, gave a right to a jury from the county where the offense had been committed (an approximation of the "vicinage" requirement), a right whose pale cousin can also be found in the Sixth Amendment right to an impartial district jury. Section 29 generally linked jury selection to the practice then prevailing in the state in which the crime had taken place.[45] In criminal cases, no appeal was provided.

In civil cases, Sections 22 and 25 allowed higher court review only by writ of error, not by the "civilian" appeal as to both law and fact. This limitation extended even to admiralty and equity cases and was not removed from them until 1803.[46] Again, the Seventh Amendment constitutionalized the jury's last word on facts by prohibiting the "reexamination" of any fact tried by a jury otherwise "than according to the rules of the common law."

Sections 16, 19, 26, and 30 limited equity jurisdiction. Section 16 was the general clause that restated the common law rule that suits in equity shall not be sustained in any case in which, as the Judiciary Act put it, "plain, adequate and complete remedy may be had at law." Since this went more or less without saying, saying it meant making a political point in favor of juries and against judicial factfinding.[47] Sections 19, 26, and 30 specifically circumscribed such fact-finding.

The Senate fought over these matters with great intensity, although only a few senators shared the abhorrence of "chancery" displayed by the Pennsylvanian William Maclay, who, in spite of the victories scored by the anti-chancery faction, alleged that the bill had broken down the bar between chancery and common law: "all actions may now be tryed in the federal Courts by Judges, without the intervention of a Jury. The Tryal by Jury is considered as the Birth right of every american, it is a priviledge they are fond of, and let me add it is a priviledge they will not part with."[48]

Senator Pierce Butler of South Carolina, in his final speech against the judiciary bill, alleged that the success of the American Revolution would be a phantom if the bill were adopted: "If the People of America Shall be Subject to two Systems of Jurisprudence to the Passions and Caprices of two Sets of Judges or Rulers their Situation is not bettered by their Success; and they have been Contending for a Phantom."[49] Similar sentiments were expressed in the House of Representatives, perhaps most articulately by Michael Stone of Maryland, who became a judge after serving in the First Congress and who said:

> I am, sir, for this Government moving as silently as death, that the people should not perceive the least alteration for the worse in their situation; the exercise of this power will certainly be the most odious that can be exercised, for mankind do not generally view courts of justice with a favorable eye, they are intended to correct the vices of the community, and consequently are disagreeable to human nature. It was well observed, and I concur in the opinion, that of all the wheels in Government, the Judicial is the most disagreeable.[50]

Although much of this opposition must be seen as "antifederalist," in the narrower sense of that word, it should also be interpreted as involving fears about the powers of the third branch as such. For the influence of these fears, we do not have to rely on roll-call analysis. We need only look at the manner in which the Judiciary Act and, to a lesser extent, the Bill of Rights deal with juries, fact-finding, review of facts, equity, and equity procedures. The main author of the finely tuned Judiciary Act, Oliver Ellsworth, certainly did not believe that the judiciary should move "silently as death," but the very control Congress asserted over court procedure, structure, and jurisdiction put the judiciary in a place that was narrower than the one allowed and, perhaps, contemplated by Article III.

Some of the provisions of the Judiciary Act regarding court structure and jurisdiction had the effect, even if not fully intended, of tempering judicial power. At the Constitutional Convention a fair amount of time had been spent discussing fixed judicial salaries, including the question of whether allowing Congress to increase salaries could be reconciled with the notion of judicial independence. Article III prohibits only the diminution of salaries. In the event, Congress' control of the court structure and its ability to impose (and lift) the burdens of circuit riding placed the judges, especially the Supreme Court justices, in a position of almost debilitating dependence. Justices John Blair, James Wilson, and James Iredell even offered to agree to a salary reduction of $500 each, if this would get Congress to attend to their problem.[51] Attorney General Edmund Randolph, in his report to the House of Representatives in

December 1790, made it clear that he thought the system had a negative effect on the quality of the third branch.[52] Ten years later, when John Jay declined a second term as Chief Justice, matters had not changed. "I left the bench perfectly convinced," he wrote to President Adams, "that under a system so defective it would not obtain the energy, weight, and dignity which are essential to its affording due support to the national government, nor acquire the public confidence and respect which, as the last resort of the justice of the nation, it should possess."[53]

When Congress, in February 1801, a few weeks after John Jay's letter to Adams and in the waning days of the Adams presidency, finally passed an act to provide for separate circuit courts with their own set of judges,[54] the independent judiciary had come to be thought of in partisan terms—as it was by Adams' successor when *his* Congress, in 1802, restored the 1789 system.[55] Thereafter Jefferson spoke about the judiciary in antifederalist terms, dreaming of "some practical & impartial" control composed of a mix of state and federal authorities.[56]

The manner in which the Judiciary Act defined the jurisdiction of the federal courts likewise had the effect of placing limitations on judicial power, although the primary issue here was probably the nature of American federalism rather than the nature of the judiciary. Apart from government litigation, admiralty, federal rights, and diversity were the important jurisdictional heads. Even the opposition agreed that the admiralty jurisdiction belonged in the hands of federal courts. Many opponents also thought that the Supreme Court at least should have the power, specified in Section 25 of the Judiciary Act, to review cases in which claims based on federal rights had been denied. Diversity jurisdiction was a more controversial subject. Since 1789, political and academic disputes over the compulsory or discretionary nature of the federal judicial power outlined in Article III[57] have obscured the fact that the First Congress withheld much less than it conferred. The Judiciary Act gave almost every jurisdictional item listed in Article III, Section 2, to some federal court. Although it conferred no general federal question jurisdiction on the lower federal courts, it did give the Supreme Court the last word, even if it was restricted to issues of law involving the denial of federal claims by state courts.

What makes it so difficult to generalize about the subject of jurisdiction is the give-and-take that Congress engaged in. The fears of those who drew up the federal judiciary in terror could partially be assuaged through compromise over jurisdictional structures and, especially, compromise over jurisdictional amounts. By setting a $2,000 minimum for writs of error in cases brought to the Supreme Court from the circuit courts and a $500 threshold for access to the circuit courts in diversity cases, the Judiciary Act went a long way toward accommodating the Aedanus Burkes of the First Congress who feared that "a man might be dragged three or four hundred miles from his home, and tried by men who know nothing of him, or he of them."[58]

As to the great French preoccupation, the power of judicial review, the First Congress treated it essentially the same way the Constitutional Convention had: influential members clearly thought that it was implicit in Article III. Section 25 made these assumptions more or less explicit. While the French thought of judicial review as violating the separation of powers, the Americans were more inclined to regard it as a necessary tool for ensuring the supremacy of the power behind the powers: the constituent power of the people. Coming out of the tradition of mixed government, they were also more inclined than the French to find virtue in a system of checks and balances. Yet in a system in which checks were heaped upon checks, Congress apparently found it to be the most natural thing in the world to assert the power to fashion the tool of judicial review by conferring and withholding jurisdiction. Only a few members believed that Congress' labors regarding jurisdiction were bound to be futile, given the possibility that the judges might invoke the sweeping text of Article III or the very concept of judicial review to overcome congressional limitations on their power.[59]

Assuming congressional power over the federal courts is not the same as saying that future Congresses would easily be able to exercise control. At least one member of Congress, Representative William Loughton Smith of South Carolina (who had briefly studied law at the Middle Temple), fully comprehended that given judicial independence, the judiciary framework Congress was constructing in the summer of 1789, once erected, would be difficult to dismantle. Since more than 200 years of history have borne him out, Smith shall have the last word. In the House debate of August 29, 1789, Smith, who was a supporter of the Judiciary Act, urged careful consideration of the question whether there should be lower federal courts, as it would "not be easy to alter the system when once established." He then went on: "After this point is settled, the next which occurs is the extent of federal jurisdiction to be annexed to this court. This question is as important as the former; for it will not be less difficult than improper to enlarge or curtail the jurisdiction of a court already established."[60] Smith was wrong about enlargement of federal court jurisdiction; he was right about its curtailment.

The members of the First Congress appreciated the importance of their undertaking as they deliberated over the judiciary and the Bill of Rights. The task of figuring out the appropriate role for the third branch in a constitutional democracy was perhaps the most puzzling of all the challenges the framers' generation faced. The Judiciary Act, more so than Article III, combined diverse conceptions of the judiciary into a whole—coherent or not—that made possible the initial acceptance of the federal courts and thus laid the foundation for their continuous development since.

NOTES

ACKNOWLEDGMENTS

INDEX

NOTES

1. THE TASK OF SEPARATING POWER

1. Philip B. Kurland, "The Rise and Fall of the 'Doctrine' of Separation of Powers," 85 *Michigan Law Review* 603 (1986). See also Louis Fisher, "The Efficiency Side of Separated Powers," 5 *Journal of American Studies* 131 (1971).

2. Kurland, "Rise and Fall," 603.

3. Peter L. Strauss, "The Place of Agencies in Government: Separation of Powers and the Fourth Branch," 84 *Columbia Law Review* 574 (1984).

4. Steven G. Calabresi, "Some Normative Arguments for the Unitary Executive," 48 *Arkansas Law Review* 28 (1995).

5. See Gerhard Casper, "Constitutional Constraints on the Conduct of Foreign and Defense Policy: A Nonjudicial Model," 43 *University of Chicago Law Review* 477 (1976).

6. McGeorge Bundy, "The Presidency and the Peace," 42 *Foreign Affairs* 353 (1964).

7. See Arthur M. Schlesinger, Jr., *The Imperial Presidency* (1973).

8. See Harry H. Wellington, *Interpreting the Constitution: The Supreme Court and the Process of Adjudication* (1990).

9. Lawrence Lessig and Cass R. Sunstein, "The President and the Administration," 94 *Columbia Law Review* 86 (1994).

10. Id. at 87.

11. Steven G. Calabresi and Saikrishna B. Prakash, "The President's Power to Execute the Laws," 104 *Yale Law Journal* 553 (1994).

12. Various conundrums of constitutionalism are put forward and analyzed in Jon Elster and Rune Slagstad, *Constitutionalism and Democracy* (1988). See also Gerhard Casper, "Constitutionalism," in 2 *Encyclopedia of the American Constitution* 473–480 (Leonard W. Levy, ed., 1986). The subtlest and most complete treatment of interpretation from a historical perspective is Jack N. Rakove, *Original Meanings* (1996).

13. I have adapted formulations applied by Ernst Gombrich to the humanities; see Ernst Gombrich, "Focus on the Arts and Humanities," 35 *Bulletin of American Academy of Arts and Sciences,* no. 4, pp. 5–7 (1982).

14. See Calabresi and Prakash, "President's Power," 570.

15. See Lessig and Sunstein, "President and the Administration," 12. See also Rakove, *Original Meanings,* 244.

16. As concerns the challenges of constitutional interpretation, I generally agree with Lessig and Sunstein at 87–89.

17. Felix Frankfurter, "Paradoxes in Legal Science," in *Felix Frankfurter on the Supreme Court: Extrajudicial Essays on the Court and the Constitution,* 203 (Philip B. Kurland, ed., 1970).

18. Jacques L. Godechot, *Les constitutions de la France depuis 1789,* 35 (1970).

19. M. J. C. Vile, *Constitutionalism and the Separation of Powers,* 184 (1967).

20. Michel Troper, *La séparation des pouvoirs et l'histoire constitutionnelle française,* 158–159 (1980).

21. W. B. Gwyn, *The Meaning of the Separation of Powers: An Analysis of the Doctrine from Its Origin to the Adoption of the United States Constitution,* 8 (1965).

22. Maryland Declaration of Rights of 1776, art. VI, in 3 *The Federal and State Constitutions, Colonial Charters, and Other Organic Laws of the States, Territories, and Colonies, Now or Heretofore Forming the United States of America,* 1687 (Francis Newton Thorpe, ed., 1909).

23. Virginia Constitution of 1776, in 7 *Federal and State Constitutions,* 3815.

24. For some of the sources, see the excerpts in 1 *The Founders' Constitution,* 311–354 (Philip B. Kurland and Ralph Lerner, eds., 1987).

25. See Gwyn, *Meaning of the Separation of Powers,* 11–27.

26. Charles de Secondat Montesquieu, 1 *The Spirit of Laws,* bk. XI, chap. 6 (J. V. Prichard, ed., rev. ed. 1991; Thomas Nugent, trans., 1st ed., 1750).

27. Compare Gwyn, *Meaning of the Separation of Powers,* 26. See also Rakove, *Original Meanings,* 251.

28. See Polybius, *The Rise of the Roman Empire,* 317–318 (Ian Scott-Kilvert, trans., 1979).

29. See Alessandro Passerin d'Entrèves, *The Notion of the State,* 115 (1967).

30. John Adams, 1 *A Defence of the Constitutions of Government of the United States of America,* 169 (1787).

31. Id. at 176.

32. In fact even the sources of governmental authority varied from one colony to another.

33. Willi Paul Adams, *The First American Constitutions: Republican Ideology and the Making of the State Constitutions in the Revolutionary Era,* 257 (1980) (quoting William Douglass, 1 *A Summary, Historical and Political, of the British Settlements in North-America,* 213–215 [1755]).

34. See Vile, *Constitutionalism and the Separation of Powers,* 128.

35. Adams, *First American Constitutions,* 259–262.

36. Gordon S. Wood, *The Radicalism of the American Revolution,* 187, 189 (1992).

37. See id. at 169; Edmund S. Morgan, *Inventing the People: The Rise of Popular Sovereignty in England and America,* 87 (1988).

38. See Kurland, "Rise and Fall," 593.

39. Morgan, *Inventing the People,* 248–249.

40. The first South Carolina constitution, which was short-lived,

vested the "legislative power" in a president, an assembly, and a legislative council, and thus provided the president with an absolute veto.

41. The New York institutional arrangements were more complex.

42. Virginia Constitution of 1776, in 7 *Federal and State Constitutions,* 3816: "according to the laws of this Commonwealth."

43. Id. at 3816–17. For a discussion of these and related restrictions and practices, see Charles C. Thach, Jr., *The Creation of the Presidency, 1775–1789: A Study in Constitutional History,* 29–34 (1969). See also Rakove, *Original Meanings,* 250.

44. Oscar Handlin and Mary Handlin, eds., *The Popular Sources of Political Authority; Documents on the Massachusetts Constitution of 1780,* 324–325 (1966).

45. Id. at 337.

46. Massachusetts Declaration of Rights of 1780, art. V, in 3 *Federal and State Constitutions,* 1890.

47. Adams, 3 *Defence of the Constitutions,* 419.

48. New Hampshire Bill of Rights of 1784, art. XXXVII, in 4 *Federal and State Constitutions,* 2457.

49. The "civil officers" were the Postmaster General after 1775, and the Secretary of Foreign Affairs, the Secretary of War, and the Superintendent of Finance after 1781. In 1784, however, the latter was to be replaced by a Board of Treasury.

50. Henry J. Bourguignon, *The First Federal Court: The Federal Appellate Prize Court of the American Revolution, 1775–1787,* 101–134 (1977).

51. See Thach, *Creation of the Presidency,* 73.

52. 3 *The Papers of Alexander Hamilton,* 420–421 (Harold C. Syrett, ed., 1966).

53. Id. at 421.

54. Id. at 420 n.l.

55. 1 *The Records of the Federal Convention of 1787,* 18 (Max Farrand, ed., rev. ed. 1966).

56. Id. at 20–21.

57. See 3 *Records of the Federal Convention,* 595–630.

58. 1 *Records of the Federal Convention,* 30–31.

59. James Madison, *The Federalist, No. 47,* 339, 337, 338 (Benjamin Fletcher Wright, ed., 1961).

60. James Madison, Amendments to the Constitution (June 8, 1789), in 12 *The Papers of James Madison,* 202 (Charles F. Hobson and Robert A. Rutland, eds., 1979).

61. 46 *Library of Congress Information Bulletin,* 350–352 (1987).

62. 1 *Annals of Congress,* 760–761 (Joseph Gales, ed., 1789).

63. Id. at 760.

64. See James Madison, Statement on the Removal Power of the President (May 19, 1789), in 12 *Papers of James Madison,* 172–174.

65. Bernard Schwartz, 2 *The Bill of Rights: A Documentary History,* 1150 (1971).

66. 1 *Records of the Federal Convention,* 106.

67. Id. at 81.

68. 2 *Records of the Federal Convention,* 301, 586–587.

69. Forrest McDonald, *Novus Ordo Seclorum: The Intellectual Origins of the Constitution,* 250 (1985).

70. 1 *Records of the Federal Convention,* 233.

71. 2 *Records of the Federal Convention,* 538.

72. Id. at 314–315, 614.

73. See William Crosskey and William Jeffrey, Jr., 3 *Politics and the Constitution in the History of the United States,* 19 (1980).

74. McDonald, *Novus Ordo Seclorum,* 262–263.

75. See Wood, *Radicalism of the American Revolution,* 187.

76. Thach, *Creation of the Presidency,* 52.

77. McDonald, *Novus Ordo Seclorum,* 258.

78. See Vile, *Constitutionalism and the Separation of Powers,* 13 (the "pure doctrine" of separation of powers is an "ideal type" that has rarely been put into practice).

79. Gwyn, *Meaning of the Separation of Powers,* 128.

80. See 1 *Annals of Congress,* 492–501 (1789).

2. THE CONDUCT OF GOVERNMENT DURING
THE WASHINGTON ADMINISTRATION

1. For one of the most extensive treatments of the first year of government under the Constitution, see James Hart, *The American Presidency in Action 1789: A Study in Constitutional History* (1948).

2. *Journal of William Maclay, United States Senator from Pennsylvania, 1789–1791* (April 30, 1789), 8–9 (2nd ed. 1927).

3. Id. (May 1, 1789) at 9 (emphasis omitted).

4. Id. at 9–10. Maclay objected to the manner in which the Chancellor of the State of New York introduced the President. The Chancellor proclaimed, " 'Long live George Washington, President of the United States!' " 1 *Annals of Congress,* 26–27 (Joseph Gales, ed., 1789).

5. *Journal of William Maclay* (May 1, 1789), 10.

6. Id. (May 9, 1789) at 25.

7. Letter from George Washington to James Madison (May 5, 1789), in 12 *The Papers of James Madison,* 132 (Charles F. Hobson and Robert A. Rutland, eds., 1979).

8. Georgia Constitution of 1777, art. XXXII, in 2 *The Federal and State Constitutions, Colonial Charters, and Other Organic Laws of the States, Territories, and Colonies, Now or Heretofore Forming the United States of America,* 782 (Francis Newton Thorpe, ed., 1909).

9. See Gordon S. Wood, *The Creation of the American Republic 1776–1787,* 144 (1969). Compare Steven G. Calabresi and Joan L. Larsen, "One Person, One Office: Separation of Powers or Separation of Personnel?" 79 *Cornell Law Review* 1045 (1994) (discussing the incompatibility clause of the U.S. Constitution).

10. *Journal of William Maclay* (June 17, 1789), 76–79.

11. See the account in George H. Haynes, 1 *The Senate of the United States: Its History and Practice,* 52–58 (1938).

12. 1 *Annals of Congress,* 65 (1789). See Haynes, 1 *Senate of the United States,* 62–68.

13. See *Journal of William Maclay* (August 22–24, 1789), 125–130.

14. See Haynes, 1 *Senate of the United States,* 68.

15. 1 *Annals of Congress,* 592 (1789).

16. Id. at 607 (statement of Rep. Sherman).

17. Forrest McDonald, *Alexander Hamilton: A Biography,* 128 (1979).

18. 1 *Annals of Congress,* 592–593 (1789) (statement of Rep. Page).

19. Id. at 593 (statement of Rep. Tucker).

20. Id. at 601 (statement of Rep. Gerry).

21. Id. at 607.

22. See 3 *Annals of Congress,* 490–494 (1792); quotation at 493.

23. Thomas Jefferson, "The Anas" (April 2, 1792), in 1 *The Writings of Thomas Jefferson,* 190 (Paul Leicester Ford, ed., 1892).

24. 3 *Annals of Congress,* 536 (1792).

25. No papers, or rather copies of papers, were withheld in this case, however.

26. 3 *Annals of Congress,* 679 (1792).

27. Id. at 680–681 (statement of Rep. Ames).

28. Id. at 683 (statement of Rep. Venable).

29. Id. at 686 (statement of Rep. Ames).

30. 14 *The Papers of James Madison,* 406.

31. Jefferson, "The Anas" (April 2, 1792), 190.

32. See Abraham D. Sofaer, *War, Foreign Affairs, and Constitutional Power: The Origins,* 79–93 (1976).

33. 3 *Annals of Congress,* 414 (1792).

34. 4 *Annals of Congress* 150 (1793).

35. Id. at 151. See Daniel N. Hoffman, *Governmental Secrecy and the Founding Fathers: A Study in Constitutional Controls,* 100–104 (1981).

36. See James Sterling Young, *The Washington Community, 1800–1828,* 6 (1966).

37. *Journal of William Maclay* (July 9, 1789), 101.

38. See F. W. Maitland, *The Constitutional History of England: A Course of Lectures,* 387–399 (1926).

39. It is much discussed in the present controversies concerning

the so-called "unitary executive." See, for instance, Lawrence Lessig and Cass R. Sunstein, "The President and the Administration," 94 *Columbia Law Review* 22 (1994); Steven G. Calabresi and Saikrishna B. Prakash, "The President's Power to Execute the Laws," 104 *Yale Law Journal* 642 (1994). The most detailed treatment is that by Hart, *American Presidency in Action,* 152. For the most recent account, see David P. Currie, "The Constitution in Congress: The First Congress and the Structure of Government, 1789–1791," 2 *University of Chicago Law School Roundtable* 195 (1995).

40. See Theodore Y. Blumoff, "Separation of Powers and the Origins of the Appointment Clause," 37 *Syracuse Law Review* 1051–57 (1987).

41. 1 *Annals of Congress,* 370–371 (1789).

42. See id. at 372–382.

43. Louis Fisher, *Constitutional Conflicts between Congress and the President,* 60–61 (1985).

44. This is the position Hamilton took. See Alexander Hamilton, *The Federalist, No. 77,* 484–489 (Benjamin Fletcher Wright, ed., 1961).

45. This suggestion was one of several put forth by Madison.

46. James Madison, "Statement on the Removal Power of the President" (May 19, 1789), in 12 *Papers of James Madison,* 174.

47. 1 *Annals of Congress,* 564–565 (1789) (statement of Rep. Stone).

48. Id. at 459 (statement of Rep. Smith).

49. Id. at 573–576 (statement of Rep. Gerry).

50. Id. at 503.

51. Id. at 505 (statement of Rep. Benson).

52. Id. at 576.

53. Id. at 578, 580.

54. Id. at 580, 585.

55. For the various Senate votes, see Fisher, *Constitutional Conflicts,* 65.

56. For a detailed analysis, see Charles A. Miller, *The Supreme Court and the Uses of History,* 205–210 (1969).

57. 1 *Annals of Congress,* 565 (1789) (statement of Rep. Stone).

58. James Madison, "Statement on the Treasury Department" (June 29, 1789), in 12 *Papers of James Madison,* 265–266.

59. Id. at 266.

60. Id. at 267.

61. Madison, "Statement on the Removal Power of the President," 172–174.

62. 1 *Annals of Congress,* 612–614 (1789).

63. Id. at 615.

64. An Act for establishing an Executive Department, to be denominated the Department of Foreign Affairs, 1 Stat. 28–29 (1789); An Act to establish an Executive Department, to be denominated the Department of War, 1 Stat. 49–50 (1789). The Department of Foreign Affairs was subsequently given additional responsibilities and in effect, once it was renamed the Department of State, became the "Home Department" that the parsimonious First Congress had rejected. On the far-reaching responsibilities of the State Department (which, in the absence of a Justice Department, included administration of the court system), see Leonard D. White, *The Federalists: A Study in Administrative History,* 128–144 (1978).

65. An Act for establishing the Salaries of the Executive Officers of Government, with their Assistants and Clerks, 1 Stat. 67 (1789).

66. An Act to establish the Treasury Department. Id. at 65–67. See generally White, *The Federalists,* 116–127 (describing Treasury operations).

67. 1 Stat. 65–66 (1789).

68. McDonald, *Alexander Hamilton,* 133.

69. New York Constitution of 1777, art. XXII, in 5 *Federal and State Constitutions* 2633.

70. 2 *The Records of the Federal Convention of 1787,* 314–315, 614 (Max Farrand, ed., rev. ed. 1966).

71. 1 *Annals of Congress,* 670–671 (1789).

72. Id. at 894–895.

73. Noble E. Cunningham, *The Process of Government under Jefferson,* 216 (1978).

74. For the most recent examination of the constitutional issues, see the thorough analysis by David P. Currie, "The Second Congress, 1793–1795," 90 *Northwestern University Law Review* 606 (1996). Currie's treatment is part of *The Constitution in Congress: The Federalist Period, 1789–1801,* (Chicago: University of Chicago Press, forthcoming in 1997).

75. Letter from Chief Justice Jay and Associate Justices to George Washington (August 8, 1793), in 3 *The Correspondence and Public Papers of John Jay,* 488–489 (Henry P. Johnston, ed., 1891).

76. Report of Secretary of State Jefferson, Submitted to Congress (December 30, 1790), in 1 *American State Papers: Foreign Relations,* 100 (Walter Lowrie and Matthew St. Clair Clarke, eds., 1833).

77. For two detailed accounts of the Algiers episode, see Ray W. Irwin, *The Diplomatic Relations of the United States with the Barbary Powers, 1776–1816* (1931); and H. G. Barnby, *The Prisoners of Algiers: An Account of the Forgotten American-Algerian War, 1785–1797* (1966).

78. Irwin, *Diplomatic Relations,* 20.

79. Id. at 28–33.

80. See Report of Jefferson to Congress (December 30, 1790), 101.

81. 2 *Annals of Congress,* 1728, 1730 (1790).

82. Message from President Washington (December 30, 1790), in 1 *American State Papers: Foreign Relations,* 100.

83. Prices ranged from $1,200 to $2,920 a man. See Report of Jefferson to Congress (December 30, 1790), 101.

84. See list in 18 *The Papers of Thomas Jefferson,* "Editorial Note" at 435–436, and "Editorial Note" at 404 (Julian P. Boyd, ed., 1971).

85. Report of Secretary of State Jefferson, Submitted to the House of Representatives (December 30, 1790) and Senate (January 3, 1791), in 1 *American State Papers: Foreign Relations,* 104.

86. Id. at 105. In the end, the opinion turned out to be exceedingly accurate.

87. Id.

88. 18 *Papers of Thomas Jefferson,* "Editorial Note" at 429–430.

89. Id. at 410, 436–437.

90. *Journal of William Maclay* (January 3, 1791), 353.

91. Committee Report on Mediterranean Trade (January 6, 1791), in 1 *American State Papers: Foreign Relations,* 108.

92. 18 *Papers of Thomas Jefferson,* 410n.

93. 2 *Annals of Congress,* 1735 (1790).

94. Message from President Washington (February 22, 1791), in 1 *American State Papers: Foreign Relations,* 128.

95. An Act making an appropriation for the purpose therein mentioned, 1 Stat. 214 (1791).

96. For a detailed account, see 18 *Papers of Thomas Jefferson,* "Editorial Note" at 410–413.

97. Hoffman, *Governmental Secrecy,* 68, 79.

98. Letter from Captain Richard O'Brien, Submitted to Congress (December 9, 1791), in 1 *American State Papers: Foreign Relations,* 130.

99. Committee Report on Mediterranean Trade (January 6, 1791), 133.

100. Thomas Jefferson, "The Anas" (March 11, 1792), 183–184 (abbreviated words spelled out).

101. Id. (April 9, 1792) at 190–191 (abbreviated words spelled out).

102. Senate Resolution (May 8, 1792), in 1 *American State Papers: Foreign Relations,* 136.

103. 1 *American State Papers: Foreign Relations,* "Editorial Note" at 290; An Act making certain appropriations therein mentioned, 1 Stat. 284–285 (1792).

104. See 1 *American State Papers: Foreign Relations,* 288–300.

105. Letter from Edward Church to the Secretary of State, Submitted to Congress (December 16, 1793). Id. at 296.

106. Message from President Washington (December 16, 1793). Id. at 288.

107. See the account in Hoffman, *Governmental Secrecy,* 100–104.

108. 4 *Annals of Congress,* 154 (1794).

109. Hoffman, *Governmental Secrecy,* 102.

110. See 1 *American State Papers: Foreign Relations,* 413–423.

111. Irwin, *Diplomatic Relations,* 60.

112. See, for example, 4 *Annals of Congress,* 481.

113. Irwin, *Diplomatic Relations,* 60.

114. Letter from Pierre Eric Skjoldebrand to David Humphreys, Submitted to Congress (March 3, 1794), in 1 *American State Papers: Foreign Relations,* 415.

115. An Act providing the means of intercourse between the United States and foreign nations, 1 Stat. 128–129 (1790).

116. An Act to continue in force for a limited time, and to amend the act intituled "An Act providing the means of intercourse between the United States and foreign nations," 1 Stat. 299–300 (1793).

117. An Act making further provision for the expenses attending the intercourse of the United States with foreign nations; and further to continue in force the act intituled, "An act providing the means of intercourse between the United States and foreign nations," 1 Stat. 345 (1794).

118. See An Act making appropriations for the support of Government, for the year one thousand seven hundred and ninety four, 1 Stat. 342–345 (1794); An Act making appropriations for the support of the Military establishment of the United States, for the year one thousand seven hundred and ninety four, 1 Stat. 346–347 (1794).

119. 15 *Papers of James Madison,* "Editorial Note" at 147.

120. Id. at 249.

121. Id., "Editorial Note" at 147.

122. An Act to provide a Naval Armament, 1 Stat. 350–351 (1794).

123. Irwin, *Diplomatic Relations,* 66.

124. These frigates were the *United States,* the *Constitution,* and the *Constellation.*

125. Irwin, *Diplomatic Relations,* 79.

126. 1 *American State Papers: Foreign Relations,* 532.

127. For the colorful details, see Barnby, *Prisoners of Algiers,* 191–198.

128. 1 *American State Papers: Foreign Relations,* 529–532.

129. Irwin, *Diplomatic Relations,* 74.

130. An Act making further provision for the expenses attending the intercourse of the United States with foreign nations; and to continue in force the act, intituled "An act providing the means of intercourse between the United States and foreign nations," 1 Stat. 487–488 (1796).

131. 6 *Annals of Congress,* 2245–46 (1797).

132. Id. at 1764.

133. Id. at 1763–67.

134. Id. at 2235.

135. Id. at 2235–45.

136. See Dumas Malone, *Jefferson, the President: Second Term, 1805–1809,* vol. 5 of *Jefferson and His Time,* 37–49 (1974).

137. Sofaer, *War, Foreign Affairs, and Constitutional Power,* 210.

138. 28 *Annals of Congress,* 269 (1815) (Message of President Madison).

139. Id. at 1943.

140. Treaty between United States and Algiers, Submitted to the Senate (December 6, 1815), in 4 *American State Papers: Foreign Relations,* 4 (Walter Lowrie and Walter S. Franklin, eds., 1834); Irwin, *Diplomatic Relations,* 176–186.

141. 30 *Annals of Congress,* 13 (1816) (Annual Message of President Madison).

142. Irwin, *Diplomatic Relations,* 186.

143. Treaty with Algiers, Submitted to the Senate (January 7, 1822), in 5 *American State Papers: Foreign Relations,* 133–134 (Asbury Dickins and James C. Allen, eds., 1858).

144. See Sofaer, *War, Foreign Affairs, and Constitutional Power,* 103–116 (the Neutrality Proclamation), 85–93.

145. Report of Jefferson to House (December 30, 1790) and Senate (January 3, 1791), 105.

146. See Instructions to John Paul Jones, Submitted to Congress

(December 16, 1793), in 1 *American State Papers: Foreign Relations,* 290–292; Instructions to David Humphreys, Submitted to the Senate (February 15, 1796), id. at 528–529.

147. See Sofaer, *War, Foreign Affairs, and Constitutional Power,* 96.

148. On Jefferson's disclosures as Secretary of State, see Dumas Malone, *Jefferson and the Ordeal of Liberty,* vol. 3 of *Jefferson and His Time,* 152 (1962).

149. Hoffman, *Governmental Secrecy,* 76.

150. Jefferson, "The Anas" (April 9, 1792), 191.

151. Id.

152. 5 *Annals of Congress,* 625, 629 (1796).

153. Id. at 759.

154. Id. at 761–762. For an account of the controversy, see Sofaer, *War, Foreign Affairs, and Constitutional Power,* 85–93.

155. Malone, *Jefferson and the Ordeal of Liberty,* 258.

156. Id. at 252.

157. 5 *Annals of Congress,* 760 (1796).

158. For a similar assessment of relations between the judiciary and Congress, see Maeva Marcus and Emily Field Van Tassel, "Judges and Legislators in the New Federal System, 1789–1800," in *Judges and Legislators: Toward Institutional Comity,* 31 (Robert A. Katzmann, ed., 1988).

159. John Locke, *The Second Treatise of Government,* chap. XII, §§146–148 (Thomas P. Peardon, ed., 1952).

160. James Madison, *The Federalist, No. 45,* 329 (Benjamin Fletcher Wright, ed., 1961).

161. 10 *Papers of James Madison,* 205.

162. New Hampshire Constitution of 1784, art. XXXVII, in 4 *Federal and State Constitutions,* 2457.

3. APPROPRIATIONS OF POWER

1. Kate Stith, "Rewriting the Fiscal Constitution: The Case of Gramm-Rudman-Hollings," 76 *California Law Review* 600 (1988).

2. The proposition is disputed by Sidak in his attack on Stith. J. Gregory Sidak, "The President's Power of the Purse," 1989 *Duke Law Journal* 1162 (1989). Most of Sidak's historical arguments rest on exceedingly slender reeds. For a recent affirmation of the proposition by the Supreme Court, see Office of Personnel Management v. Richmond, 496 U.S. 414 (1990).

3. F. W. Maitland, *The Constitutional History of England: A Course of Lectures,* 309 (1926).

4. William Blackstone, 1 *Commentaries,* 296–297 (1765–1769 and facsimile ed., 1979).

5. An Act for Granting Royall Ayd, 1664 and 1665, 16 and 17 Car. 2, chap. 1.

6. An Act for Raising Moneys, 1666, 18 and 19 Car. 2, chap. 1, §33.

7. John Brewer, *The Sinews of Power,* 143 (1989).

8. An Act for a Grant, 1688, 1 W. and M., Sess. 2, chap. 1.

9. Brewer, *Sinews of Power,* 151. Although Parliament constantly thwarted fiscal policy under William, parliamentary opposition rarely succeeded after 1702. Id. at 149. Albert Gallatin made the point polemically in a speech to the House of Representatives in March 1798: "It is during that period [i.e., after the Revolution of 1688] that a progressive patronage, and a systematic, corrupting influence have sunk Parliament to a nominal representation, a mere machine, the convenience used by Government for the purpose of raising up supplies; the medium through which the Executive reaches with ease the purse of the people." 7 *Annals of Congress,* 1133 (1798).

10. See Andrew C. McLaughlin, *A Constitutional History of the United States,* 15 (1935).

11. Edwin J. Perkins, *The Economy of Colonial America,* 190 (2nd ed. 1988).

12. Davis Rich Dewey, *Financial History of the United States,* 17–18 (1924).

13. Perkins, *Economy of Colonial America,* 161–162.

14. For the term "fiscal constitution" see Kenneth W. Dam, "The

American Fiscal Constitution," 44 *University of Chicago Law Review* 271 (1977).

15. 1 *The Complete Anti-Federalist,* 53 (Herbert J. Storing, ed., 1981).

16. Many of the first state constitutions contained more or less elaborate provisions about taxation. The most intriguing of these was Section 41 of the Pennsylvania Constitution of 1776, which prohibited taxation except if it led to a better deployment of resources—almost a public goods approach to taxation: "the purpose for which any tax is to be raised ought to appear clearly to the legislature to be of more service to the community than the money would be, if not collected; which being well observed, taxes can never be burthens." 5 *The Federal and State Constitutions, Colonial Charters, and Other Organic Laws of the States, Territories, and Colonies, Now or Heretofore Forming the United States of America,* 3090–91 (Francis Newton Thorpe, ed., 1909).

17. Maitland, *Constitutional History of England,* 182, 247, 310.

18. Maryland Constitution of 1776, art. XIII, in 3 *Federal and State Constitutions,* 1692.

19. Pennsylvania Constitution of 1776, §20, in 5 *Federal and State Constitutions,* 3088.

20. South Carolina Constitution of 1778, art. 16, in 6 *Federal and State Constitutions,* 3252.

21. Maryland Constitution of 1776, art. XI, in 3 *Federal and State Constitutions,* 1692–1693.

22. See Virginia Bill of Rights of 1776, §15, in 7 *Federal and State Constitutions,* 3814.

23. New Hampshire Constitution of 1784, art. XXXVI, in 4 *Federal and State Constitutions,* 2457.

24. 3 *The Records of the Federal Convention of 1787,* 149–150 (Max Farrand, ed., rev. ed. 1966).

25. See Jennings B. Sanders, *Evolution of Executive Departments of the Continental Congress, 1774–1789,* 50–74, 126–152 (1935).

26. An Act to Establish the Treasury Department, 1 Stat. 65 (1789).

27. 1 *Annals of Congress,* 231–232 (Joseph Gales, ed., 1789).

28. Id. at 670–671.

29. The House did not establish a standing Committee on Ways and Means until 1795.

30. 1 *Annals of Congress,* 894–895 (1789).

31. 5 *The Papers of Alexander Hamilton,* 381–392 (Harold C. Syrett, ed., 1962).

32. 1 Stat. 95 (1789). In this chapter I focus exclusively on the annual appropriations. In addition to appropriations for the ongoing operations of government, there were special appropriations, supplemental appropriations, and legislation dealing with government debt.

33. The classic treatment of these matters is Lucius Wilmerding, Jr., *The Spending Power: A History of the Efforts of Congress to Control Expenditures* (1943), especially chap. 2.

34. 6 *Papers of Alexander Hamilton,* 129–136.

35. Id. at 280.

36. 1 Stat. 104–105 (1790).

37. Id. at 105.

38. 2 *Annals of Congress,* 1449 (1790) (statement of Rep. Livermore).

39. Id. at 1450 (statement of Rep. Bland).

40. *The Diary of William Maclay and Other Notes on Senate Debates* (March 22, 1790), vol. 9 of *Documentary History of the First Federal Congress,* 226 (Kenneth R. Bowling and Helen E. Veit, eds., 1988).

41. 6 *Papers of Alexander Hamilton,* 282; Wilmerding, *Spending Power,* 22.

42. 1 Stat. 190 (1791).

43. For an account from a Hamiltonian perspective, see Forrest McDonald, *Alexander Hamilton: A Biography,* 237 (1979).

44. 9 *Papers of Alexander Hamilton,* 456–475.

45. For a description of the practices, see Wilmerding, *Spending Power,* 26.

46. 19 *Papers of Alexander Hamilton,* 402. The observation is a

part of Hamilton's elaborate "explanation" of the system of anticipations, 400–427.

47. 3 *Annals of Congress,* 221–229 (1791).

48. 9 *Papers of Alexander Hamilton,* 475.

49. See 1 Stat. 226–229 (1791).

50. Jefferson still debated this issue as late as 1804. See letter from Thomas Jefferson to Albert Gallatin (February 19, 1804), in 11 *The Writings of Thomas Jefferson,* 4–13 (Andrew A. Lipscomb, ed., 1903).

51. 1 Stat. 325–328 (1793).

52. 3 *Annals of Congress,* 890 (1791).

53. Letter from Jefferson to Gallatin (February 19, 1804), 13.

54. See the detailed account in 13 *Papers of Alexander Hamilton,* "Introductory Note" at 532.

55. Albert Gallatin, A Sketch of the Finances of the United States, in 3 *The Writings of Albert Gallatin,* 111 (Henry Adams, ed., 1879, reprint 1960).

56. 14 *Papers of Alexander Hamilton,* 27.

57. McDonald, *Alexander Hamilton,* 260.

58. 13 *Papers of Alexander Hamilton,* 541 n.20.

59. 3 *Annals of Congress,* 899 (1793).

60. Id. at 901.

61. For an explanation, see Leonard D. White, *The Federalists: A Study in Administrative History,* 328 n.18 (1978).

62. For a critical assessment of this move, see Dumas Malone, *Jefferson and the Ordeal of Liberty,* vol. 3 of *Jefferson and His Time,* 188–190 (1962).

63. Gallatin, *Sketch of Finances,* 117. See also 1 Stat. 404 (1793).

64. Gallatin, *Sketch of Finances,* 118.

65. See Edwin G. Burrows, *Albert Gallatin and the Political Economy of Republicanism, 1761–1800,* 452 (1986).

66. Raymond Walters, Jr., *Albert Gallatin: Jeffersonian Financier and Diplomat,* 3–4 (1957).

67. See the excellent account in Burrows, *Gallatin and Political Economy of Republicanism,* 467–493.

68. Walters, *Albert Gallatin*, 89.

69. 1 Stat. 498–501, 508–509 (1797). The adverb "respectively" is the very term employed by the 1666 Act of Parliament quoted earlier.

70. 6 *Annals of Congress*, 2040 (1797); compare Gallatin, *Sketch of Finances*, 116. For a detailed account of Gallatin's struggle with the new Treasury Secretary, Oliver Wolcott, see Wilmerding, *Spending Power*, 28–49. Gallatin was not a zealot and understood the need for a reasonable discretion: "The most proper way would perhaps be not to enter so many details . . . but to divide the general appropriation under a few general heads only, allowing thereby sufficient latitude to the executive officers of government, but confining them strictly, in the expenditure under each of those general heads, to the sum appropriated by law." Gallatin, *Sketch of Finances*, 117. See also House Report on Applications of Public Money (April 29, 1802), in 1 *American State Papers: Finance*, 752–757 (Walter Lowrie and Matthew St. Clair Clarke, eds., 1832).

71. See 1 Stat. 542 (1798) and 1 Stat. 717 (1799).

72. 1 Stat. 563 (1798).

73. See 2 Stat. 62 (1800) and 2 Stat. 117 (1801). See also White, *The Federalists*, 329.

74. Burrows, *Gallatin and Political Economy of Republicanism*, 486.

75. 7 *Annals of Congress*, 1121–22 (1798).

76. 8 *Annals of Congress*, 1317–18 (1798).

77. 24 *Papers of Alexander Hamilton*, 31.

78. See Gallatin, *Sketch of Finances*, 118.

79. Malone, *Jefferson and the Ordeal of Liberty*, 188.

80. 1 *A Compilation of the Messages and Papers of the Presidents, 1789–1897*, 425–430 (James D. Richardson, ed., 1896).

81. Noble E. Cunningham, *The Process of Government under Jefferson*, 56 (1978) (quoting Attorney General Rodney).

82. 17 *Annals of Congress*, 818–830 (1807) (statement of Rep. Randolph).

83. Id. The additional appropriations were voted. 2 Stat. 450 (1807).

84. 17 *Annals of Congress,* 830 (1807) (statement of Rep. Smilie).

4. JEFFERSON'S "SHACKLES OF POWER"

1. Thomas Jefferson, First Inaugural Address (March 4, 1801), in 1 *A Compilation of the Messages and Papers of the Presidents, 1789–1897,* 322 (James D. Richardson, ed., 1896). For a brief summary of the major Republican positions, see Abraham D. Sofaer, *War, Foreign Affairs, and Constitutional Powers: The Origins,* 68–69 (1976).

2. On the major problems and positions regarding divided government since World War II, see David R. Mayhew, *Divided We Govern: Party Control, Lawmaking, and Investigations, 1946–1990,* 1–6 (1991).

3. Charles Warren, 1 *The Supreme Court in United States History,* 193 (rev. ed. 1926) (citing letter from Thomas Jefferson to Joel Barlow, March 14, 1801).

4. 2 Stat. 89 (1801), repealed by "An Act to repeal certain acts respecting the organization of the Courts of the United States; and for other purposes," 2 Stat. 132 (1802).

5. See Richard E. Ellis, *The Jeffersonian Crisis: Courts and Politics in the Young Republic,* 234–242 (1971).

6. Letter from John Jay to John Adams (January 2, 1801), in 4 *The Correspondence and Public Papers of John Jay,* 285 (Henry P. Johnston, ed., 1893).

7. Letter from Thomas Jefferson to Judge Spencer Roane (September 6, 1819), in 10 *The Writings of Thomas Jefferson,* 140 (Paul Leicester Ford, ed., 1899).

8. Compare Jay Fliegelman, *Declaring Independence: Jefferson, Natural Language, & the Culture of Performance,* 160 (1993) (describing the "dialectical" nature of the word "revolution").

9. Thomas Jefferson, "The Anas" (October 1, 1792), in 1 *Writings of Thomas Jefferson,* 203.

10. Fliegelman, *Declaring Independence,* 140.

11. Jefferson, "The Anas" (October 1, 1792), 204.

12. Samuel Eliot Morison, Henry Steele Commager, and William E. Leuchtenburg, 1 *The Growth of the American Republic,* 331 (7th ed. 1980).

13. Jefferson, First Inaugural Address (March 4, 1801), 321–322 (emphasis added).

14. 15 *Annals of Congress,* 561 (1806) (statement of Rep. Randolph).

15. John W. Reps, *Monumental Washington: The Planning and Development of the Capital Center,* 22 (1967).

16. Id. at 17 and 20.

17. Report from Major Pierre L'Enfant to President George Washington (June 22, 1791), in *L'Enfant and Washington,* 55 (Elizabeth S. Kite, ed., 1929).

18. James Sterling Young, *The Washington Community, 1800–1802,* 6 (1966).

19. Id. at 8.

20. Reps, *Monumental Washington,* 21.

21. Memorandum from Paul Turner, Professor, Stanford University Art Department, to Gerhard Casper (January 5, 1994) (on file with author).

22. Dumas Malone, *Jefferson, the President: First Term, 1801–1805,* vol. 4 of *Jefferson and His Time,* 91 (1970).

23. Journal of William Maclay (May 1, 1789), in *The Journal of William Maclay,* 10 (2d ed. 1927).

24. Letter Accompanying President Thomas Jefferson's First Annual Message to Congress (December 8, 1801), in 8 *Writings of Thomas Jefferson,* 108 n.1 (1896).

25. Letter from Thomas Jefferson to Dr. Benjamin Rush (December 20, 1801), id. at 127–128.

26. Noble E. Cunningham, *The Process of Government under Jefferson,* 25 (1978) (quoting letter from Nathaniel Macon to Thomas Jefferson, April 20, 1801, microfilmed on 23 Presidential Papers Microfilm: Thomas Jefferson Papers 19198, Library of Congress).

27. Id. at 26 (quoting letter from Michael Leib to Lydia Leib, December 9, 1801, on file with Leib-Harrison Family Papers, Miscellaneous Collection, Historical Society of Pennsylvania, Philadelphia).

28. See Fliegelman, *Declaring Independence,* 38–39.

29. Id. at 4, 5.

30. Georgia Constitution of 1777, art. XXXII, in 2 *The Federal and State Constitutions, Colonial Charters, and Other Organic Laws of the States, Territories, and Colonies, Now or Heretofore Forming the United States of America,* 782 (Francis Newton Thorpe, ed., 1909).

31. Fliegelman, *Declaring Independence,* 93–94 (quoting letter from John Adams to Benjamin Rush, December 25, 1811, in *The Spur of Fame: Dialogues of John Adams and Benjamin Rush, 1805–1813,* 201–202 [John A. Schutz and Douglass Adair, eds., 1966]) (alterations in Fliegelman).

32. Alexander Hamilton, "The Examination No. 1," *New York-Evening Post* (December 17, 1801), in 25 *The Papers of Alexander Hamilton,* 453 (Harold C. Syrett, ed., 1977) (work widely attributed to Alexander Hamilton, though signed with pen name Lucius Crassus).

33. Letter from Jefferson to Rush (December 20, 1801), 127.

34. Malone, *Jefferson, the President: First Term,* 98.

35. Thomas Jefferson, First Annual Message (December 8, 1801), in 8 *Writings of Thomas Jefferson,* 118.

36. See Cunningham, *Process of Government under Jefferson,* 48–49.

37. Sofaer, *War, Foreign Affairs, and Constitutional Powers,* 209–210 (citing Order from Samuel Smith, for the Acting Secretary of the Navy, to Captain Richard Dale, May 20, 1801, in 1 *Naval Documents Related to the United States Wars With the Barbary Powers: Naval Operations Including Diplomatic Background from 1785 Through 1801,* 465 [U.S. Navy Department, ed., 1939]).

38. Letter from Thomas Jefferson to James Madison, Secretary of

State (September 12, 1801), in 8 *Writings of Thomas Jefferson,* 94.

39. Hamilton, "The Examination No. 1," 454–455.

40. Notes on President's Message from Albert Gallatin to Thomas Jefferson (December 1802), in 1 *The Writings of Albert Gallatin,* 105 (Henry Adams, ed., 1879, reprint 1960).

41. Cunningham, *Process of Government under Jefferson,* 49–50.

42. Notes on President's Message from Gallatin to Jefferson (December 1802), 105–106.

43. Sofaer, *War, Foreign Affairs, and Constitutional Power,* 214.

44. Act of February 6, 1802, chap. 4, 2 Stat. 129, 130 (1802), quoted id. at 215.

45. Id. at 210.

46. Report of Secretary of State Jefferson, Submitted to the House of Representatives (December 30, 1790), and to the Senate (January 3, 1791), in 1 *American State Papers: Foreign Relations,* 105 (Walter Lowrie and Matthew St. Clair Clarke, eds., 1833).

47. Sofaer, *War, Foreign Affairs, and Constitutional Power,* 225.

48. Id. at 226 (arguing that if Jefferson had been more like Hamilton or Gallatin, "he would have been able to carry out most if not all his plans without constitutional inconsistency and embarrassment").

49. Jefferson, First Annual Message (December 8, 1801), 120–121.

50. "Gallatin displayed moderation, industry, eloquence, integrity, a genius for administration and finance, a painstaking attention to detail, a mastery of parliamentary tactics, an enlightened humanitarianism and a broad and farsighted conception of democracy." Henry Steele Commager, "Gallatin, Albert," in 6 *Encyclopaedia of the Social Sciences,* 549 (Edwin R. A. Seligman, ed., 1931).

51. Cunningham, *Process of Government under Jefferson,* 79.

52. Notes on President's Message from Gallatin to Jefferson (December 1802), 68.

53. Alexander Hamilton, "The Examination No. 11," *New York-*

Evening Post (February 3, 1802), in 25 *Papers of Alexander Hamilton*, 514, 516.

54. Communication from the Secretary of the Treasury to the Chairman of the Committee, Appointed to Investigate the State of the Treasury in Answer to the Enquiries Made by the Committee, 8, 18 (1802), microprint in Early American Imprints, 2d Series, Shaw-Shoemaker Bibliography, 1801–1819, no. 3264, American Antiquarian Society, Worcester, Mass.

55. Id. at 19.

56. House Bill of April 8, 1802, 7th Cong., 1st sess., sec. 1 (1802), microfilmed on 7th Congress 1801–1803, 1st Session and 2nd Session (Library of Congress) (emphasis added); compare Cunningham, *Process of Government under Jefferson*, 115 (stating that although the itemization was not noticeably greater, members of the House viewed it as a departure from previous practice). The bill is an example of "framework legislation," which is both declaratory and regulatory in nature. Framework legislation, unlike ordinary legislation, regulates congressional and executive branch decision-making. See Gerhard Casper, "Constitutional Constraints on the Conduct of Foreign and Defense Policy: A Nonjudicial Model," 43 *University of Chicago Law Review* 482 (1976). Contemporary examples include the Congressional Budget and Impoundment Control Act of 1974, Pub. L. No. 93–344, 88 Stat. 297 (1974) (codified in scattered sections of various titles of U.S.C.) (establishing new procedures for Congress to control impoundment of funds by the executive branch); and the War Powers Resolution, Pub. L. No. 93–148, 87 Stat. 555 (1973) (codified at 50 U.S.C. §§1541–48 [1988]) (creating procedures for the President and Congress to use the armed forces).

57. Act of May 1, 1802, chap. 46, §1, 2 Stat. 183 (1802) (emphasis added). The term "enacting clause" refers to the formulaic language used in appropriations bills to introduce each individual appropriation; thus an enacting clause may be used to indicate the specificity with which an appropriation is in-

tended to be employed. See Leonard D. White, *The Jeffersonians: A Study in Administrative History 1801–1829*, 112 (1956).

58. Act of March 2, 1801, chap. 18, §1, 2 Stat. 109 (1801) (emphasis added); Act of May 1, 1802, chap. 18, §1, 2 Stat. at 183 (1802) (emphasis added).

59. Letter from Albert Gallatin to Thomas Jefferson (January 18, 1803), in 1 *Writings of Albert Gallatin,* 117.

60. Letter from Albert Gallatin to Thomas Jefferson (October 13, 1806), id. at 310.

61. White, *The Jeffersonians,* 51.

62. Cunningham, *Process of Government under Jefferson,* 217.

63. 15 *Annals of Congress,* 1019–20 (1806) (statement of Rep. Williams).

64. Id. at 1020 (statement of Rep. Dana).

65. Id. at 1021.

66. Id. at 1063 (statement of Rep. Randolph).

67. See 19 *Annals of Congress,* 347–352, 1330–31 (1809).

68. See Cunningham, *Process of Government under Jefferson,* 115–117.

69. Letter from Albert Gallatin to Representative G. W. Campbell (February 4, 1809), microformed on *The Papers of Albert Gallatin,* Roll 18, RG56 (Rhistoric Publications, Philadelphia).

70. Act of December 22, 1807, chap. 5, 2 Stat. 451 (1807) (laying an embargo on all foreign goods), repealed by Act of March 1, 1809, chap. 24, §19, 2 Stat. 533 (1809).

71. 19 *Annals of Congress,* 1554 (1809) (statement of Rep. Alston).

72. Act of March 3, 1809, chap. 28, §1, 2 Stat. 535 (1809) (regulating the Treasury, Navy, and War departments) (emphasis added).

73. See Hamilton, "The Examination No. 11," 516–517.

74. Id. at 514–515.

75. See Malone, *Jefferson, the President: First Term,* 102.

76. See Cunningham, *Process of Government under Jefferson,* 58.

77. My understanding of Madison in this regard has been influenced by James P. O'Rourke, "James Madison and the Ex-

tending Republic, 1780–1820" (Honors thesis, Harvard University, 1991).

78. Thomas Jefferson, Second Annual Message (December 15, 1802), in 8 *Writings of Thomas Jefferson*, 183.

79. 12 *Annals of Congress*, 280–281 (1802) (House Resolution), 314–323, 325–339 (1803).

80. Id. at 340 (House Resolution).

81. Id. at 359 (statement of Rep. Dana).

82. Id. at 373–374 (report of the committee charged with evaluating the proposed appropriation).

83. The Senate vote was a narrow fourteen to twelve. See id. at 104.

84. William Plumer Junior, ed., *Life of William Plumer*, 255–256 (1857), quoted in Everett Somerville Brown, *The Constitutional History of the Louisiana Purchase: 1803–1812*, 13 (1920).

85. See Gerhard Casper, "Comment: Government Secrecy and the Constitution," 74 *California Law Review* 924–925 (1986).

86. For a comprehensive account, see Malone, *Jefferson, the President: First Term*, 284–332.

87. Irving Brant, *James Madison: Secretary of State 1800–1809*, 126 (1953).

88. 12 *Annals of Congress*, 255 (1803) (Senate Resolution); see Brant, *James Madison*, 126.

89. Brant, *James Madison*, 132.

90. Malone, *Jefferson, the President: First Term*, 284.

91. Id. at 302.

92. Thomas Jefferson, Third Annual Message (October 17, 1803), in 8 *Writings of Thomas Jefferson*, 268, 269.

93. 13 *Annals of Congress*, 382 (1803) (message of President Jefferson).

94. Id. at 385 (statement of Rep. Griswold).

95. 5 *Annals of Congress*, 759–762 (1796).

96. 13 *Annals of Congress*, at 338–339 (1803) (statement of Rep. Randolph).

97. Id. at 392 (statement of Rep. Smilie).

98. Id. at 419.

99. Cunningham, *Process of Government under Jefferson,* 274.

100. Malone, *Jefferson, the President: First Term,* 327.

101. Remarks on President's Message from Albert Gallatin to Thomas Jefferson (October 4, 1803), in 1 *Writings of Albert Gallatin,* 156.

102. Jefferson, Third Annual Message (October 17, 1803), 266 n.1 (Madison's notes of October 1, 1803, on a draft of Jefferson's message) (abbreviated words spelled out).

103. 13 *Annals of Congress,* 487, 498 (1803) (quoting the Senate bill).

104. Id. (statement of Rep. Randolph).

105. Id. at 500 (statement of Rep. Griswold).

106. Letter from Rev. Manasseh Cutler to Rev. Dr. Dana (November 30, 1803), in 2 *Life, Journals and Correspondence of Rev. Manasseh Cutler, LL.D.,* 148 (William Parker Cutler and Julia Perkins Cutler, eds., 1988), quoted in Brown, *Constitutional History of Louisiana Purchase,* 89.

107. Everett Somerville Brown, ed., *William Plumer's Memorandum of Proceedings in the United States Senate, 1803–1807,* 27 (1923), quoted in Brown, *Constitutional History of Louisiana Purchase,* 89.

108. 13 *Annals of Congress,* 545 (1803) (Senate Resolution).

109. Id. at 511 (statement of Rep. Jackson).

110. Thomas Jefferson, Drafts of an Amendment to the Constitution (July 1803), in 8 *Writings of Thomas Jefferson,* 247 n.1 (quoting letter from Jefferson to Wilson Cary Nicholas, September 7, 1803).

111. Id. at 244 n.1 (quoting letter from Jefferson to John C. Breckenridge, August 12, 1803).

112. Letter from Thomas Jefferson to John B. Colvin (September 20, 1810), in 9 *Writings of Thomas Jefferson,* 279 (1898).

113. Jefferson, Drafts of an Amendment to the Constitution (July 1803), 244 n.1 (quoting letter from Jefferson to Breckenridge, August 12, 1803).

114. Massachusetts Constitution of 1780, art. V, in 3 *Federal and State Constitutions,* 1890.

115. Thomas Jefferson, "The Anas" (October 1, 1792), 203; see also letter from Thomas Jefferson to James Monroe (May 20, 1782), in 3 *Writings of Thomas Jefferson,* 56–60 (expressing Jefferson's distaste for public life).

116. Letter from Thomas Jefferson to P. S. Dupont de Nemours (March 2, 1809), in *Thomas Jefferson: Writings,* 1203 (Merrill D. Peterson, ed., 1984) .

5. THE JUDICIARY ACT OF 1789
AND JUDICIAL INDEPENDENCE

1. 1 Stat. 73 (1789).

2. *Legislative Histories: Amendments to the Constitution through Foreign Officers Bill,* vol. 4 of *Documentary History of the First Federal Congress of the United States of America, 1789–1791,* 45–48 (Charlene Bangs Bickford and Helen E. Veit, eds., 1986).

3. Articles of Amendment (August 24, 1789), id. at 39.

4. Jacques Leon Godechot, ed., *Les constitutions de la France depuis 1789,* 35 (1970).

5. Decree of August 4–11, 1789, in 1 *Collection complète des lois, décrets, ordonances, règlements, et avis du Conseil-D'Etat,* 39 (J. B. Duvergier, ed., 1824).

6. See John P. Dawson, *The Oracles of the Law,* 305–373 (1968).

7. Decree of August 16–24, 1790, in 1 *Collection complète,* 361. The provisions were reiterated in the first of the postrevolutionary French constitutions, that of September 3, 1791. See Godechot, *Constitutions de la France,* 58. See also Decree of November 27–December 1, 1790, in 2 *Collection complète,* 65 (constituting the Court of Cassation "at" the legislative branch).

8. Decree of August 16–24, 1790, title II, art. 13, 363.

9. See Massachusetts Declaration of Rights of 1780, arts. IV and V, in 3 *The Federal and State Constitutions, Colonial Charters, and Other Organic Laws of the States, Territories, and Colonies, Now or Heretofore Forming the United States of America,* 1890 (Francis Newton Thorpe, ed., 1909).

10. 12 and 13 Will. Ill. c. 2. On the earlier history, see Alfred F. Havighurst, "The Judiciary and Politics in the Reign of Charles II" (pts. 1 and 2), 66 *Law Quarterly Review* 62, 229 (1950).

11. Declaration of Independence (July 4, 1776), in *Sources of Our Liberties: Documentary Origins of Individual Liberties in the United States Constitution and Bill of Rights,* 320 (Richard L. Perry, ed., 5th ed., 1972).

12. Massachusetts, New Hampshire, New York, Delaware, Maryland, Virginia, North Carolina, and South Carolina. The remaining states provided for terms ranging from one to seven years.

13. Massachusetts, New Hampshire, Pennsylvania, Maryland, and South Carolina (1776 and 1778). Delaware followed suit in 1792.

14. Connecticut, Rhode Island, New Jersey, Pennsylvania, and Georgia (1776). For a discussion of developments in the individual states, see Martha Andes Ziskind, "Judicial Tenure in the American Constitution: English and American Precedents," *Supreme Court Review* 138–147 (1969).

15. This was also the case in Connecticut, Rhode Island, Delaware (joint ballot of president and General Assembly), New Jersey, and South Carolina. Georgia judges were popularly elected.

16. Massachusetts, New Hampshire, New York, Pennsylvania, and Maryland gave the appointment power to the governor and a variously constituted council. See generally William S. Carpenter, *Judicial Tenure in the United States* (1918).

17. Massachusetts Declaration of Rights of 1780, art. XXIX, 1893.

18. New Hampshire Bill of Rights of 1784, art. XXXVII, in 4 *Federal and State Constitutions,* 2457.

19. Gordon S. Wood, *The Creation of the American Republic, 1776–1787*, 301 (1969).

20. Massachusetts Declaration of Rights of 1780, art. XXIX, 1893.

21. See Gerhard Casper, "Constitutionalism," in 2 *Encyclopedia of the American Constitution*, 479 (Leonard W. Levy, ed., 1986).

22. 2 *The Records of the Federal Convention of 1787*, 428–429 (Max Farrand, ed., rev. ed. 1966).

23. Id. at 34.

24. James T. Barry III, "Comment: The Council of Revision and the Limits of Judicial Power," 56 *University of Chicago Law Review* 253 (1989).

25. Maeva Marcus and Natalie Wexler, "The Judiciary Act of 1789: Political Compromise or Constitutional Interpretation?" in *Origins of the Federal Judiciary: Essays on the Judiciary Act of 1789*, 18 (Maeva Marcus, ed., 1992).

26. 1 *Records of the Federal Convention*, 124.

27. 1 *Annals of Congress*, 813 (Joseph Gales, ed., 1789).

28. Id. at 807.

29. Massachusetts Declaration of Rights of 1780, art. V, 1890.

30. Notes of William Paterson (June 23, 1789), in *The Diary of William Maclay and Other Notes on Senate Debates*, vol. 9 of *Documentary History of the First Federal Congress of the United States of America, 1789–1791*, 478 (Kenneth R. Bowling and Helen E. Veit, eds., 1988); 1 *Annals of Congress*, 805 (1789) (statement of Rep. Sedgwick); id. at 806–808 (statement of Rep. Ames); id. at 828–829 (statement of Rep. Gerry).

31. 1 *Annals of Congress*, 799 (1789) (statement of Rep. Smith).

32. "Essays of Brutus," *New York Journal* (March 20, 1788), in 2 *The Complete Anti-Federalist*, 438 (Herbert J. Storing, ed., 1981).

33. Id.

34. This last clause was added on August 27, 1787, probably to clarify that the Supreme Court would continue to have the full range of appellate powers in non-common-law fields such as admiralty—in the language of the time often referred

to as "civil" law. See 2 *Records of the Federal Convention,* 431.
The federal judicial power was extended to equity by another
floor amendment virtually without discussion, also on August 27. Id. at 428.

35. 3 *The Debates in the Several State Conventions on the Adoption
of the Federal Constitution as Recommended by the General
Convention in Philadelphia in 1787,* 205 (Jonathan Elliot, ed.,
1876). Ralph Lerner has noted that "no moderately sensitive
reader of *The Federalist, No. 78,* can overlook the defensive
character of its rhetoric." Ralph Lerner, "The Supreme Court
as Republican Schoolmaster," *Supreme Court Review* 167 n.119
(1967).

36. 3 *Debates in the Several State Conventions,* 519.

37. "Essay of a Democratic Federalist," *Pennsylvania Herald* (October 17, 1787), in 3 *Complete Anti-Federalist,* 60. On the history of equity in Pennsylvania before the Revolution, see
Stanley N. Katz, "The Politics of Law in Colonial America:
Controversies over Chancery Courts and Equity Law in the
Eighteenth Century," in *Colonial America: Essays in Politics
and Social Development,* 409–414 (Stanley N. Katz, ed., 2nd
ed., 1976).

38. *Diary of William Maclay* (July 1, 1789), 96.

39. Charles de Secondat Montesquieu, 1 *The Spirit of Laws,* bk.
XI, chap. 6 (J. V. Prichard, ed., rev. ed. 1991; Thomas Nugent,
trans., 1st ed. 1750).

40. "Letters of Centinel," *Independent Gazetteer,* Philadelphia,
and *Freeman's Journal,* Philadelphia (October 1787–April
1788), in 2 *Complete Anti-Federalist,* 136.

41. Sounding exasperated, Hamilton had to devote all of *The
Federalist, No. 83,* to the "disingenuous" objection that the
silence of the Constitution in regard to civil juries represented
an abolition of trial by jury. Alexander Hamilton, *The Federalist, No. 83,* 518 (Benjamin Fletcher Wright, ed., 1961).

42. "Essays by a Farmer," *Maryland Gazette* (March 21, 1788), in
5 *Complete Anti-Federalist,* 38–39.

43. Charles Warren, "New Light on the History of the Federal Judiciary Act of 1789," 37 *Harvard Law Review* 53 (1923).

44. Id. at 79.

45. Julius Goebel, Jr., *Antecedents and Beginnings to 1801*, vol. 1 of *The Oliver Wendell Holmes Devise History of the Supreme Court of the United States*, 506–507 (1971).

46. An Act in addition to an act intituled "An act to amend the judicial system of the United States," 2 Stat. 244 (1803). See Warren, "New Light," 102–103.

47. See Warren, "New Light," 97; Goebel, *Antecedents and Beginnings*, 500.

48. *Diary of William Maclay* (July 13, 1789), 109.

49. Id. at 455.

50. 1 *Annals of Congress*, 827 (1789).

51. Maeva Marcus and Emily Field Van Tassel, "Judges and Legislators in the New Federal System, 1789–1800," in *Judges and Legislators: Toward Institutional Comity*, 48 (Robert A. Katzmann, ed., 1988).

52. Report of the Attorney-General, Submitted to the House of Representatives (December 31, 1790), in 1 *American State Papers: Miscellaneous*, 23–24 (Walter Lowrie and Walter S. Franklin, eds., 1834).

53. Letter from John Jay to John Adams (January 2, 1801), in 4 *The Correspondence and Public Papers of John Jay*, 285 (Henry P. Johnston, ed., 1893).

54. An Act to provide for the more convenient organization of the Courts of the United States, 2 Stat. 89 (1801).

55. An Act to repeal certain acts respecting the organization of the Courts of the United States; and for other purposes, 2 Stat. 132 (1802). On the subject generally, see Richard E. Ellis, *The Jeffersonian Crisis: Courts and Politics in the Young Republic* (1971).

56. Thomas Jefferson, *Autobiography* (January 6, 1821), in *Thomas Jefferson: Writings*, 74 (Merrill D. Peterson, ed., 1984).

57. See, for example, William R. Casto, "The First Congress's

Understanding of Its Authority over the Federal Courts' Jurisdiction," 26 *Boston College Law Review* 1101 (1985).

58. 1 *Annals of Congress,* 812 (1789).

59. The position taken by Elbridge Gerry. Id. at 829. Gerry was not a lawyer by background. But Edmund Randolph also suggested that this was a possibility. Letter from Edmund Randolph to James Madison (June 30, 1789), in 12 *The Papers of James Madison,* 274 (Charles F. Hobson and Robert A. Rutland, eds., 1979).

60. 1 *Annals of Congress,* 797–798 (1789).

ACKNOWLEDGMENTS

My interest in separation of powers issues was first stimulated by my former colleague at the University of Chicago and friend, for three decades, Philip B. Kurland. Phil Kurland died in 1996. Few constitutional scholars of this century have as consistently as Phil Kurland thought and worried about the Constitution as a complex system that cannot be reduced to one of its components. Phil Kurland and two other Chicago colleagues and friends, David Currie and Cass Sunstein, each in his own way, encouraged me in my pursuits and supported me through debate and criticism. Stanley N. Katz, in his Chicago days, guided me on historiographic issues. I am also indebted to my Stanford colleague Gerald Gunther, who for decades treated me as his colleague even before I became one formally.

I had three research assistants to whom I owe more than an ordinary debt. At the University of Chicago Law School, my initial foray into the primary materials, for teaching purposes, was ably facilitated by Chester Paul Beach, a member of the law school class of 1980. James P. O'Rourke, who graduated from Stanford Law School in 1995, provided most helpful research assistance for the Jefferson chapter. Leslie Hatamiya, third-year law student at Stanford, provided criticism and was most constructive in pulling it all together. At Chicago I had the friendly support of Marlene Vellinga as my secretary. Ingrid Deiwiks, executive secretary to the president of Stanford, works miracles and manages to keep more balls in the air at any given moment than anybody else I have known. My thanks to all of them.

The essays in this book originated with an invitation to give a historical paper at a separation of powers conference at the College of William and Mary in 1988. That effort whetted my curiosity about appropriations. The opportunity to give the Ben J. Altheimer Lecture at the University of Arkansas in 1990 allowed me to pursue the subject further. The question of what happened to the appropriations process after the opposition took over the government in 1801 and an interest in Thomas Jefferson that goes back to my days at the Yale Law School underlay my 1994 Jefferson Memorial Lecture at the University of California at Berkeley. I was enabled to go beyond my primary interest in executive-congressional relations when I was asked to deliver the keynote address (at the Supreme Court) of the Bicentennial Conference on the Judiciary Act of 1789 in 1989. How the judiciary was seen in the vigorous debate over what was an appropriate separation of the powers in a republican form of government was a question that cannot fail to interest any teacher of U.S. constitutional law.

Much of the text of these interconnected essays, though inevitably modified, has been previously published. I am grateful for permission to reuse "An Essay in Separation of Powers: Some Early Versions and Practices," 30 *William and Mary Law Review* 211 (1989), © 1989 by the College of William and Mary; "Appropriations of Power," 13 *University of Arkansas Law Journal* 1 (1990), © 1990 by the Board of Trustees of the University of Arkansas; "Executive-Congressional Separation of Power during the Presidency of Thomas Jefferson," 47 *Stanford Law Review* 473 (1995), © 1995 by the Board of Trustees of the Leland Stanford Junior University; and "The Judiciary Act of 1789 and Judicial Independence," in *Origins of the Federal Judiciary: Essays on the Judiciary Act of 1789,* 281 (Maeva Marcus, ed., 1992), © 1992 by Oxford University Press.

INDEX